PEAK PERFORMANCE

How Denver's Peak Academy is saving millions of dollars, boosting morale and just maybe changing the world. (And how you can too!)

By Brian Elms with J.B. Wogan

GOVERNING MANAGEMENT SERIES

Governing Books, Washington, DC

Published by Governing Books
A division of *Governing* magazine
1100 Connecticut Ave. NW, Suite 1300
Washington, DC 20036

www.governing.com

ISBN: 978-0-9833733-5-3

CONTENTS

This book is dedicated to all the men and women who work tirelessly on improving the lives of others. Innovate. Elevate. Repeat

Oh, and for Kora, who shines a bright light for the future.

FOREWORD

I believe that you are only as good as your team. During my time on the Denver City Council, I saw areas all across city government that were inefficient or outdated, areas where small changes to a single process could greatly improve city operations and residents' experiences. Governments everywhere face similar challenges. As I investigated ways to bring about a transformation to make those improvements, there were a few key themes that kept coming up that were clearly standing in the way of meaningful innovation.

For many years, Denver outsourced most of our innovating to outside consultants. But that just reinforced the idea that government, and city employees in particular, wasn't capable of innovating on its own, which simply isn't true. We also made the error of asking for input but then failing to follow through on the ideas. Finally, we equated IT with innovation, which resulted in undue pressure put on the IT department to be the sole driver of innovating on behalf of the rest of the city, leaving the rest of our employees to believe that it wasn't their place.

When I began to delve deeper into process improvement, a lightbulb went off for me. I realized that successful innovation must start with the people who actually do the work. So as one of my first acts as mayor, I established Peak Performance and the Peak Academy. Instead of outside experts telling city workers how to do their jobs better, Peak invests in employees by giving them the tools to solve problems themselves.

Today, improvements in people and processes are the cornerstone of Denver's innovation strategy. And Brian Elms has been integral to that evolution. His zeal and positivity for his work are infectious. As you'll read, establishing Peak Academy wasn't an easy task. Not everyone shares Brian's enthusiasm for continuous improvement. Not every employee or manager wants to change or admit that how they're doing something could be done better. But over time, Brian and his team have transformed how city agencies operate, how we approach customer service, and how employees think and go about their work.

While Brian has led the charge, I wish there were some way that all our employees could collectively have written this book with him. After all, this is about them. Our continued investment in our colleagues is paying huge dividends for the residents of Denver. One obvious way we see this is shorter wait times at counters. We teach ourselves that waste is disrespectful to both employees and customers. I don't know of a better way to show we mean it than by reducing the time our customers wait in line for a marriage license, permit, food voucher or vehicle registration. We're lowering wait times across the city not by adding more staff, but by removing unnecessary and redundant steps. This book is about everyone who chose to invest in themselves through Peak Academy, and especially those who acted on their ideas. I want to thank each and every one of them for finding a way to get it done.

Lastly, I'm thankful to the Peak Academy team for their humble efforts to embed and support innovation in Denver's city government. Brian and the rest of the team come from diverse backgrounds, with different mindsets, personalities and attitudes—and it makes all the difference, as you'll find out in this book. This movement is about people, not methodology. And it takes special people to do this work, striking a fine balance between "fishing" and "teaching to fish."

Dozens of governments from around the nation and world have participated in Peak Academy, and we learn as much from them as they do from us. The key message I hope Peak trainees and readers of this book take away is that continued investment in your people is the key to innovation.

Mayor Michael B. Hancock
City and County of Denver

DISCLAIMER

Writing this book may get me into trouble. There will be people who read it in hopes of finding some juicy tidbit they can use to discredit me or Denver Mayor Michael Hancock. There will be people who do not believe in government who will say, "Look how dumb these bureaucrats are! This is why government should not exist." The day we release this book, we are opening ourselves up for a barrage of criticism from skeptics, naysayers and jerks.

Don't get me wrong, I like critics. They can help you improve. But if you want to critique the Peak Academy program, please target our work, not the people we highlight or the mayor. The mayor is making himself vulnerable by allowing us to print real stories about process improvement in government. In process improvement, it's easy to be proud of the end result, but it takes courage to talk about the way things were and why they needed to change. In this book, I discuss the importance of having champions in process improvement, and Mayor Hancock is one of our champions. By letting me write a book, he has taken a chance on me and my team—one that most mayors wouldn't take. Not many public servants get to write a book and keep their job while doing it. Most have to wait until they've changed jobs, and even then they usually have to resort to using generalized examples and fake names of city workers.

In this book, you'll notice that the good stories are really specific.

The stories of failure are more broad. I highlight failures because I want to give an insider's honest take of how government works, and what we can do to make it better—not because I want to rake some employee or some department over the coals. (And don't get too excited about the failures: I didn't include stories about employees breaking the law or violating ethics rules. No one's going to rob a bank in here.)

So do me a favor. Read this book in the same spirit, recognizing the value of failure and with an eye on how to improve your own organization.

Another disclaimer: For obvious reasons, I'm writing this book in my own voice. But I wish somehow it could collectively have been written by the whole Peak team, or by all Denver employees together. I'm humbled by the successes the city's workers have achieved, and I'm thrilled to have the chance to tell this story. But please understand I know it's not my story alone to tell. (And to that end: Know that proceeds from this book are going to Denver employees, so we can keep innovating and initiating new ideas.)

Today, you can find a library full of books about innovation, and even about innovation in city government. Plenty of smart people have already written about what innovation is and how it works. We read those books and we like those books (see our Peak Academy reading list on p. 103), but that's not what this book is about. We want to tell you how to borrow the ideas and tools that are already available for free and apply them in a real-world government context. We'll give concrete examples of actual people and the situations they encountered while trying to apply the lessons of Peak. By the end, we hope that you have a recipe to start your own Peak Academy, or at least incorporate some of its lessons into your work and life.

These stacks of parking labels were hopelessly inefficient—until one Peak grad found a better way.

CHAPTER 1

JUST WHAT IS THIS 'PEAK' THING?

The city of Denver was out of ideas.

To save money during the Great Recession, the city had instituted week-long furloughs and laid off staff. It had increased employee pension contributions and raised the share that employees paid for health benefits. The government eliminated performance bonuses, froze pay and froze hiring.

It left us in a precarious situation. We weren't facing fiscal insolvency, but through all those cost-cutting measures, we had drawn down on another valuable good in our organization: employees' trust. Morale was at an all-time low. Many of our public safety departments—police, fire, the sheriff's office—didn't have the resources to hire a recruiting class. That was the environment I entered when I joined the city's performance office in 2012. I was part of a new team tasked with striking a difficult balance: Even after all the cuts, we were still facing an $80 million shortfall, but Mayor Michael Hancock wanted to find the savings without taking any more from his workforce.

Typically, the City and County of Denver solves this sort of problem the same way a lot of cities and counties do: by hiring outside consultants. A team of private-sector specialists descends on the city to assess the daily workflow of a department. These specialists, often with limited experience working in government, highlight waste, file a report recommending what business practices to change, and then head back out of town. And we all know what usually happens next: The consultants' report collects dust on a shelf, and the city itself is at a loss on how to act upon the ideas outlined in it.

Denver wanted to do things differently. My bosses in the budget office, Brendan Hanlon, David Edinger and Scotty Martin, came up with a plan to have the city solve its *own* problems, using its own employees. We would take the skills used by consultants and give them to regular city workers, so *they* would be responsible for identifying problems, proposing solutions and—here's the best part—making sure those ideas actually happened. To impart those skills, we started an in-house training and consulting program, which we called the Peak Academy. Even though the tools we teach borrow largely from established disciplines, such as lean manufacturing, we aren't beholden to any one school of thought. We don't care whose good ideas we use, so long as they lead to innovation. And our curriculum is always evolving.

I'll tell you all about how Peak works in a minute. But first let's start with a real-world example of what we're talking about.

In 2012, Jerraud Coleman was a 28-year-old window cashier working in the parking enforcement office. Jerraud had noticed a problem with the process for giving out parking permits. A resident would apply online for a neighborhood permit, and then the city would mail her a notice that she could come pick up her parking decal at city hall. She'd arrive, hand over her driver's license to Jerraud behind the window, and he'd find the appropriate decal. Then the resident would merrily skip off to go legally park her car to her heart's content.

That was the idea, anyway. But often, that simple transaction went off course. There are a couple reasons why. For starters, Jerraud and the other parking cashier had a dozen six-inch stacks of stickers sitting on top of a label that specified their designated neighborhood. But to verify that the stickers matched the right neighborhood, Jerraud had to either peel back each sticker or lift up each stack every time. Because of that dysfunctional layout, Jerraud and the other cashier had two choices: Take extra time to verify that each sticker matched the neighborhood, or risk a mistake. When they made mistakes, customers returned angry, often with parking tickets that they then had to appeal, which took even more time and more paperwork. If the cashiers instead took extra time to verify the neighborhood, the permit line could snake all the way into the lobby of city hall. Both scenarios were stressful, and the cashier position had a high turnover rate.

Jerraud's problem would feel familiar to a lot of city workers. We're not talking about grand philosophical conundrums here. Often it's just a small matter of disorganization that leads to lost time and stress. But the end result is just as profound: A simple transaction that affects 16,000 residents each year is broken, leading to unhappy citizens and city employees who don't feel good about their work.

Jerraud took Denver's week-long Peak Academy intensive training and then returned to work with a solution he wanted to try, along with two other initiatives he had come up with for other inefficiencies in the parking office.

What was his big fix for the permit problem? A label. He added a label above each stack so that he and his colleague wouldn't have to take an extra step to verify that the stack actually corresponded to the right neighborhood.

Jerraud's solution may seem obvious to you, but I guarantee that within your own organization, you have dozens of similar inefficiencies that no one has ever taken the time to rethink and solve. Normally, we as public-sector employees are too busy trying to meet the daily demands of the job to examine small tweaks that might have a big impact.

The change Jerraud proposed cost nothing (okay, $5 worth of sticky notes). And it wouldn't warrant a front-page story in the newspaper. But think about this: Let's say it takes Jerraud one minute every time he has to locate the right parking permit. That's 16,000 minutes a year, or 267 hours, or six weeks' worth of work. I don't know what Jerraud was making at that time, but let's say it was around $25 per hour, the average for a Denver city employee. That's a grand total of $6,675. That means we were paying Jerraud more than $6,000 a year to go look for stickers. And the label solution didn't just save money. It saved time for the customers and reduced the error rate on parking permits. Fewer errors meant fewer irate citizens with parking tickets to appeal. What's more, the reduced stress of the job might lead to less turnover among permit cashiers.

Employees like Jerraud are all over the city. The small-bore solutions proposed by the Jerrauds of Denver don't sound ambitious, but consider what might happen if several thousand city workers—from parking enforcement to the police department to animal protection—all had the same training and introduced the same sorts of solutions to save time and money while improving the quality of service. Suddenly, it doesn't sound so small bore.

After participating in the Peak program, Jerraud earned himself a promotion and became the Public Works employee of the year. We were so impressed with him that we invited him to become a fellow with the Peak Academy for three months. That went so well, we recruited him to become a full-time process improvement professional on our team. As he acquired new skills, his pay and responsibilities increased. Although not every trainee becomes a full-time process improvement specialist like Jerraud, many follow his general arc: After taking the class, they return to their home organization and flourish because the city has invested in them. They receive accolades, pay bumps and promotions. Of course, it's a mutually beneficial relationship. Much of the time, the initial city investment in training pays for itself when employees implement their ideas. But unlike the recession-era fixes, we're not saving money by taking things away from our staff.

There's a concept that Stephen M.R. Covey talks about in his book *Speed of Trust*, something he calls the employee trust bank. By improving efficiency and saving money without cutting back on our employees' resources, we were finally putting value back in the employee trust bank.

PEAK BY THE NUMBERS:

700
Number of employees who have finished a five-day training

4,300
Number of employees who have completed a four-hour training or participated in an improvement event

2,000+
Number of innovations submitted by Denver employees

$15M+
Amount of money saved by Peak trainees in four years

$1.2M+
Annual budget for the Peak Academy

9
Number of people who work for Peak

— as of April 2016

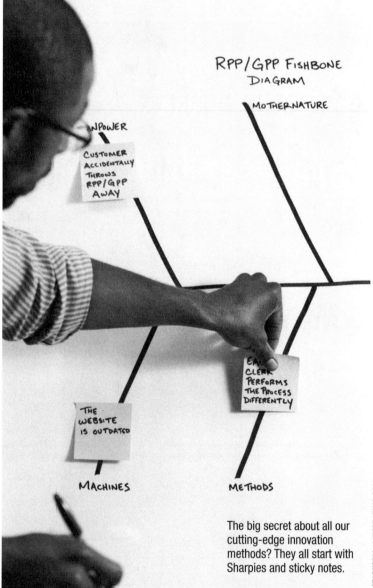

The big secret about all our cutting-edge innovation methods? They all start with Sharpies and sticky notes.

CHAPTER 2
THE NITTY AND THE GRITTY

Now that you have an idea of the impact that Peak training can have, let's talk about how the program itself actually works. The last thing I want is for this book to read like a textbook. But I do want to provide the specifics of how we structure the program to help those of you who might want to implement a similar approach in your own workplace.

First, you need to know that beyond all the techniques we teach, our goal is to make our training fun and hard. Think back to your favorite class in high school or college—not the one where you got the easy A, but the one where you learned something you still use today. If you're going to create a program like Peak, that same love is what should drive your curriculum. Don't think about lame skills workshops and compliance trainings you've sat through over the last few years. Make your training so different, so fun, so challenging, people will actually remember it.

Okay, now, what exactly is Peak? It is a process improvement organization. That means we look at the business process in government and we train frontline employees and mid-level managers how to eliminate waste and deliver better value to the customer. Think of Peak as an incubator of fresh thinking and creative problem solving within Denver government. We have nine members on the Peak team. The "academy" part of our name comes from trainings we offer.

Our trainings break down into four categories.

- **Four-hour introductory process improvement trainings.** We call these Green Belt trainings, and you actually receive a green Peak lanyard after attempting at least one innovation. Team members learn about process mapping, waste identification and the concept of standard work, loosely defined as the most efficient way to perform a task in a reproducible way.
- **Five-day process improvement trainings.** This is really the core of the academy. We call these Black Belt trainings (and yes, we hand out black lanyards to graduates who perform an innovation). Here, team members learn a slew of tools to identify and eliminate waste. They also use A3 thinking, a structured problem-solving model pioneered by Toyota, throughout their innovation experiments.
- **Executive trainings.** We offer a six-hour training to help executives understand what it's like to have process improvers in an organization.
- **Leader and supervisor trainings.** We provide one-hour courses on how to coach, run standard work and create production boards—a tool for visualizing and managing workflow.

In addition to trainings, we perform Rapid Improvement Events, or what people in lean management call "Kaizens." We also perform shorter workshops because we found many people cannot come off the floor for five days. Our workshops take one day, but in some cases we space out an eight-hour workshop into shorter segments over several weeks. With the Kaizens and workshops, we send a process improvement specialist from my team to guide a conversation and offer advice. The agency's employees, not my team, pick the problems they want to address and the solutions they want to try.

We also may engage with an agency for a longer period of time, spending up to a year working with a single organization on an innovation plan. We call this consulting relationship a Peak Partnership, and a member of my team actually sets up an office within the department and embeds for the entire duration. For all intents and purposes, they become part of the organization. (We'll discuss Peak Partnerships in greater detail on p. 61.)

Let's dive deeper into the way we structure the weeklong Peak trainings. We pack a lot into those four-and-a-half workdays. If you want to know exactly what we teach Denver employees, you can find a detailed, day-by-day curriculum on our website, available for free at denvergov.org/peakacademy.

But here I'll go over a couple of the most important techniques and exercises we teach and how they relate to Peak's larger philosophy about innovation.

On the first day of the class, we introduce the A3 model, which comes from the lean manufacturing model perfected by Toyota. (It's called an A3 because that's the name of metric paper size roughly equivalent to 11 inches by 17 inches, the largest piece of paper that will fit in a standard printer.) It's a structured approach to planning and problem solving. We like the A3 model because it forces people to reflect on what they want to fix, what exactly isn't working, and what changes might make a difference. Even if you've never heard of lean or an A3, you've probably seen someone in your life employ this kind of approach to problem solving. The A3, as we teach it, breaks into nine steps.

To illustrate the nine steps, let's imagine you are Jerraud from Chapter 1.

Step 1: State why change is needed. Residents are coming to pick up their residential parking permit and it is taking you too long to serve them. The real "why" in this case is simple. Your process shouldn't require the customer to come in person to pick up a sticker.

Step 2: Explain the current state. Some 16,000 residents a year are coming to pick up a sticker to park in their neighborhood. The stacks of stickers are tall and unorganized, which causes errors. You and your coworkers have to walk around looking for the right sticker, which causes a longer transaction.

Step 3: Explain your desired future state. In the future, residents should receive these stickers in the mail, or pick them up in a short, error-free transaction at the counter.

Step 4: Gap analysis. You now need to look for reasons why the future state isn't the current state. Treat this stage like a scientist investigating a problem in a lab. Even if you think you already know the answer, make some observations and form some hypotheses. We give our students a few ways to form a hypothesis. All of them boil down to visual representations of the process, allowing you to see more clearly where the problem might be occurring.

One tool we teach is process mapping. To continue with our parking sticker example, you would illustrate every step in the process of the residential parking program. From the perspective of the parking technician, it'd go something like this:

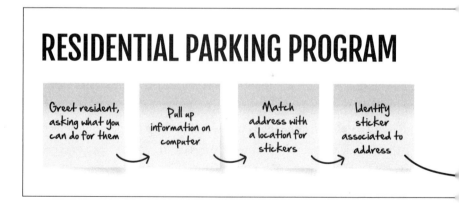

RESIDENTIAL PARKING PROGRAM

Greet resident, asking what you can do for them

Pull up information on computer

Match address with a location for stickers

Identify sticker associated to address

Process maps are great when you're trying to find ways of speeding up a process. Usually, you can do an analysis of your process map to show which steps the customer would value, and which ones he would not. Then—*presto!*—you eliminate some steps not important to the customer and improve the speed with which you deliver something. (Okay, it usually isn't that simple—some steps that the customer would call "waste" would be considered "necessary" by regulators. But you get the idea.)

However, in the case of the residential parking permit, the problem isn't just a matter of speed. There seems to be a design flaw that needs fixing, too. So you might try another tool called a fishbone diagram. Here, you draw a horizontal line with six diagonal lines branching out. At the far end, you write your problem: "Search for correct sticker." Each of the six diagonal lines represents a different category of potential causes of your printing problem: environment, methods, measurements, materials, machines and people. For this example, you'd write down a number of potential causes under each category. Under "environment," you might write that the stickers are not labeled or that they are in huge piles. The idea is to be exhaustive: List every possible problem. Later on, you can winnow the causes to the ones you think are most likely to need your attention.

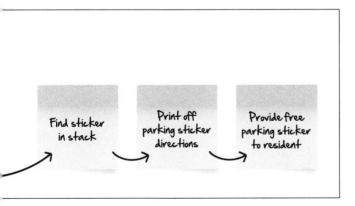

Find sticker in stack

Print off parking sticker directions

Provide free parking sticker to resident

PARKING PERMIT FISHBONE DIAGRAM

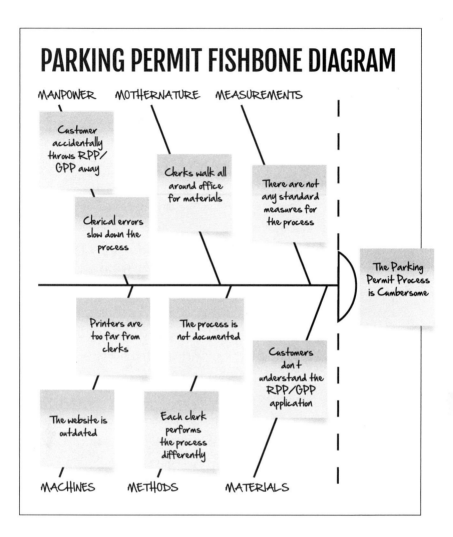

MANPOWER   MOTHERNATURE   MEASUREMENTS

Customer accidentally throws RPP/GPP away

Clerks walk all around office for materials

There are not any standard measures for the process

Clerical errors slow down the process

The Parking Permit Process is Cumbersome

Printers are too far from clerks

The process is not documented

Customers don't understand the RPP/GPP application

The website is outdated

Each clerk performs the process differently

MACHINES   METHODS   MATERIALS

Step 5: Brainstorm. Here, you run through a simple exercise. Draw a table with two columns and several rows. At the top of the left column, write "If we …." At the top of the right column, write "Then we…." In this case, you might write, "If we label the stickers, then we might be able to avoid errors and reduce the time it takes to find the right sticker." On another row, you might write, "If we find a way to mail the stickers, then we provide our customer with the right sticker in the right neighborhood."

The brainstorming part of the A3 is the first time people move from analyzing problems to proposing solutions. People tend to be stronger with one skill than the other. Some people are really great at pointing out flaws, but they don't know how to fix them. Other people are really excited about making things work, but they don't have the patience to think carefully about the root causes of a problem. The best innovations involve both, which is why it's so valuable to collaborate as a team on these issues.

BRAINSTORMING	
If We …	**Then We …**
label the stickers	might be able to avoid errors and reduce the time it takes to find the right sticker
find a way to mail the stickers	provide our customer with the right sticker in the right neighborhood

Step 6: Experiments. Draw another table with two rows. This time, at the top of the left column, write "Innovation/action." At the top of the right column, write "Actual outcome." For example, you might write that you placed labels on all the sticker stacks and in the last month no errors took place.

EXPERIMENTS	
Innovation/Action	**Actual Outcome**
Placed labels on all the sticker stacks	In the last month no errors took place

Step 7: Action plan. This is where you list the experiments you conducted, in what order and when. Create a table with three columns. The first column is for action items. The second column is for the person who gets assigned the action item. The third column is for when the action takes place. For example, you might write, "work with parking team on mailing stickers to residents ... assigned to Brian Elms ... completed on January 2, 2017."

ACTION PLAN		
Action Item	**Assigned To**	**Date Completed**
work with parking team on mailing stickers to residents	assigned to Brian Elms	completed on January 2, 2017

Step 8: Results. In this section you write down how you have progressed over the past months, providing data on errors and time it takes to perform the transaction. Here you would calculate if you were able to save any time for you or for your customer.

Step 9: Lessons learned. Create one more table with two columns. On the left, write "What went well." On the other side, write "What didn't go well." This is your opportunity to reflect on the experiments you ran and their impact. Sometimes these insights lead people to set up new experiments and a new action plan. For example, maybe the labels weren't large enough to read quickly and easily, or maybe you ran into trouble pulling addresses to mail the resident directly. Maybe you struggled calculating how long it took to provide each transaction and therefore couldn't come up with any savings.

LESSONS LEARNED	
Went Well/Helped	What Didn't go Well/Hindered
new labels helped locate the right sticker	the labels weren't large enough to read quickly and easily
	struggled to calculate how long it took to provide each transaction

What we like about the A3 is that it follows a logical progression: Identify problems, analyze problems, propose solutions, experiment with potential solutions, and evaluate the results. That logical process rests on a foundation of sound information.

But first, you must collect that information. And to do that, perhaps the most important tool we teach is something called a Gemba walk. "Gemba" is a Japanese word for "the real place," and a Gemba walk is simply a way for you to experience another employee's process firsthand.

On the second day of Peak training, we break the class into small groups and send them with an instructor out on a field trip to a Denver agency that has asked for Peak's help. The idea behind a Gemba walk is that you have to witness a process in motion before you can propose effective changes. For example, members of our class might sit with an eligibility technician in human services for two hours to see how she does her job. Then the groups reconvene in our classroom, and use the A3 model to identify opportunities to remove waste in the process. (They stop at the stage where they suggest possible solutions.) In the afternoon, employees from the host agencies come to our classroom and hear presentations from our trainees. (Our hypothetical eligibility technician would probably come along with her supervisor.)

I like every part of the Gemba walk, but I love the presentations. Here's why: For much of the weeklong training, participants are in a safe space and can say whatever they want about their boss and co-workers. They can be crude and direct and undiplomatic. But after the training, when they return to their departments, they'll have to discuss their ideas with their colleagues in a well-intentioned and rational way. The presentation part of the Gemba walk is practice for that. It creates humility, and it reinforces the fact that successful change management requires effective communication and empathy. You must balance your desire to improve your workplace with the desire not to hurt your fellow workers. Put another way: It's difficult to innovate when you're a jerk.

At the end of the week, we actually make the employees go through the presentation experience again, except this time we have them present personal ideas about their own work. Their own supervisors are invited to our classroom, and each person in our class runs through an "ignite" presentation. With assistance from Peak instructors, they prepare a five-minute PowerPoint meant to encapsulate three things they think should change in their own work. They can be as small as responding to emails faster, or as big as eliminating a wasteful task that affects hundreds of employees in the same line of work. The ignite talks give my team an early opportunity to collaborate with employees on some innovation ideas. After building that initial rapport with my team, Black Belts are more likely to keep in touch and seek help in executing their innovations.

Before the Black Belts ever leave our class, they've learned that a key element to innovation is making a compelling case for change. If you can't convince people that change is needed, you won't get very far.

At first, not everybody thought Peak was a good idea. Those early days could be long and lonely.

CHAPTER 3
RED BOUNCY-BALL CRAP

One night during the first year of the program, I turned to my wife and asked if she'd be okay if I was unemployed for a while. "I don't think I can keep doing this," I said. At that point, the experiment that would become the Peak Academy wasn't going well. Not many people were signing up for our trainings. When we did teach classes, many of them were combative. There were some exceptions, but a lot of employees didn't trust us and didn't want our help.

It's important to understand how unwelcome the Peak program initially was, because you may find the same reception when you try to innovate in your workplace. My team collects and saves feedback from our trainings, so I still have people's reasons for why they didn't believe in our program and didn't want to work with us. Here are some examples from those early days:

"Just because you work for the mayor doesn't mean we care."

"That may work at Public Works, but that will never work here."

"My boss would never let me do that."

"I'm an innovator. All I *do* is fix stuff. I just don't think my job can be fixed."

"I don't have any power or authority to do anything."

"I've been working here for more than 20 years. This red bouncy-ball crap you are teaching isn't going to work."

And it wasn't just frontline employees. Their bosses didn't want them at the trainings either. In their eyes, having an employee out for special training just meant more work for everybody else. Managers refused to send employees for a four-hour class, let alone a full week of training. I spent the first three months of my job going door to door, meeting with about a dozen department directors to ask if they would send some of their staff to our new training program. Stupidly, I had thought this would be easy, or at least easier than it was. Before coming to the budget office, I'd been a lobbyist for Denver International Airport, and, in my own estimation, a pretty good one. During my time as a lobbyist, I had already developed relationships with directors in several city departments. Besides, I was selling something that I figured they would already want: a way to teach their employees how to be innovators.

Only two directors said yes.

We saw Peak as a way to invest in our employees again after years of cuts in pay, benefits and staffing. We wanted to earn back employees' trust, and we thought we could do that by teaching new skills. Department heads didn't see it that way. They were understandably afraid that "process improvement" was a euphemism for more cuts. It all sounded like a distraction, another management fad. In hindsight, it makes sense. We were selling them an unproven product. Why wouldn't they be skeptical?

Back when I talked to my wife about quitting, I was exhausted and ready to leave. I didn't see how things could get better. We were trying to do something we believed in, and we were met with hostility at every turn. It wore us down. A couple of my original team members left within the first year. So before you launch a Peak-like program, remember: Everyone likes the idea of spreading innovation, but what that really means is long hours, lots of confrontational meetings, angry emails from trainees and their bosses, inevitable moments of self-doubt, and no guarantee that you'll be thanked for your hard work in the end.

Still on board? Good, me too. There's a reason I'm still here at Peak, in spite of that rough start. It got better—a lot better. We started with small victories. Remember, most department directors had turned us down, but two hadn't. And there's a reason why they hadn't: prior relationships. One of my bosses in the budget office, Scotty Martin, had previously worked with Denver Human Services. And as I mentioned, my prior job had been with Denver International Airport. As a favor to us, directors in both agencies promised to send a handful of employees each for our initial trainings. Without their help, the Peak Academy never would have gotten off the ground.

So we started small. We got a few additional agency directors to agree to undergo an abbreviated four-hour course to at least become familiar with the core concepts and tools we teach. Later on, some of them would encounter a work issue that reminded them of Peak, and they'd send a couple of their employees to take our training. Slowly, our Green Belts and Black Belts would return to their departments and begin using simple tools—process maps, production boards, fishbone diagrams—at their desks. Their coworkers would become interested in learning those tools and volunteer for the training.

Somewhere along the way we had our first big success. I think that's when we knew we were going to be okay. It was in the first few months, before Scotty and I had even hired other trainers. Two Green Belts from one of our first trainings, Loretta Bennion and Amber Vancil, worked at Denver Wastewater Management. They had identified a potential money-saving opportunity in their department, and they implemented it once they finished their training. You see, Wastewater was sending out warning notices whenever the city was about to put a lien on a property for late payments. They were sent using certified mail, which costs about $4.50 per notice. Bennion and Vancil switched the notices to regular postage, a simple change that saved the city an estimated $40,000 a year.

It was a big moment for us. We had been preaching the power of these various improvement techniques, but here was concrete evidence. It felt like validation, and it helped in our classes too. We could point to their innovation and tell trainees that they, too, could make this kind of impact: an immediate $40,000 in savings, simply by stopping an unnecessary practice.

Near the end of our second year, we gathered momentum. The trainings became an advertisement for more trainings. Now, we're regularly overbooked months in advance.

Today we have a long list of inspiring achievements by our graduates, and it's been a powerful tool in overcoming people's initial skepticism. Demonstrable results mean more than the fanciest Power-Point presentation we could ever give. Those results show department heads that what we're doing isn't a management fad, because it's not about the managers. It's about the employees. And that's when they stop calling your program crap. Well, some of them anyway.

There's another very important element that's helped us get through the tough times: political leadership. It certainly helped that the mayor wanted to see us succeed. Department heads want to support the boss's pet projects, and we were lucky enough to be one of those.

We've also had crucial support from Denver's Budget Director, Brendan Hanlon. Over the last four years, Brendan has received countless complaints and phone calls about me or someone on my team. These phone calls have come from HR, the city attorney, the ethics office and other high-ranking officials. Brendan never wavered in his support of me and my team. He took the complaints seriously, and he made sure we did too. But he always had our back.

We at Peak intend to help, but some managers see the program as a threat.

Look, if we're doing our job right, we're going to bring change. Change that you may think is unnecessary. Change that you think is just a euphemism for discarding a process you valued. If nothing else, our very presence in your office means someone—your boss, your coworkers, the mayor—thinks we could be doing better. In reality, process improvement is about changing practices, not people. It's difficult for some people to see the difference. It's not personal, but to them it feels deeply personal. So they lash out.

In our Black Belt training, we talk about the importance of identifying a champion you can depend on, someone who will help you try to innovate. It could be a coworker or a supervisor. When we ask Black Belts who they expect will be their champion, they often say a spouse or relative. It's great to have family members who support you, but for your innovation to succeed, you need a champion at work, too. Brendan is our champion.

The Peak Academy itself is an innovation and one that comes with real risks. For all of our success stories, know that we have critics in the city, people who see us as intrusive, mean or even detrimental to their work. Critics have tools at their disposal to stop your innovation, or at least try. A champion has to weigh critics' concerns against the merits of what you're trying to accomplish. Unfortunately, the champion's job is made all the more difficult because we won't always succeed. We might disrupt an office with good intentions, and then not achieve the giant cut in wait times or the millions in savings that would seem to justify people's initial discomfort. What happens then? If you're a potential champion, will you assume the risk, as Brendan did? If you don't, you'll have fewer complaints, but you'll have less innovation, too.

Delicious frozen yogurt.
Not pictured: Any actual improvement
in delivering city services.

CHAPTER 4
FORGET THE FRO-YO

A couple years ago, Denver's Excise and Licenses Department had an average wait time of three hours, which would sometimes stretch as long as eight hours. So the department came up with an idea: To appease the frustrated citizens waiting for hours on end, Excise and Licenses installed a frozen yogurt machine in the waiting room. You have to hand it to them: It was a clever notion. Everyone loves frozen yogurt! The move drew positive media coverage and even a customer service award from *The Denver Post*.

But the whole thing drove me nuts. Why the hell would we think we could just give people dessert and they'd put up with our horrible service?

When Stacie Loucks was appointed to the department in 2014, she decided to focus on the wait times, not frozen yogurt. Each morning, her staff would open the doors for business and immediately have a 45-minute wait. Employees at the counter were burned out, but they didn't want to leave coworkers in the lurch by taking time off. In a previous position with the mayor's office, Stacie had taken the Peak Academy training, and she knew that process improvement techniques could address many of the underlying problems in her department. The first day on the job, she called Peak and asked for our help.

Help came in two forms. We invited some of her employees to take our classes. At the same time, we appointed a Peak instructor to work regularly with Excise and Licenses staff. While we could give them tools to analyze with a fresh perspective, it would still be their insights and their success (or failure).

Loucks' team came up with dozens of ideas. The one I still love came from Leo Lopez, a license technician. One of our facilitators went on a Gemba walk, where she sat with Leo for the day to document every step in his daily work process. One client came up to the desk and handed Leo paperwork, but unlike most applications, the paperwork was in perfect order and included all the documents needed to get a security guard license. Baffled by how organized the customer was, Leo asked him where'd he gotten all his files. "My company gave it to me in this folder," the applicant said, "and told me to keep it all in order."

Leo decided to borrow the company's time-saving idea. He developed packets for each type of business license the city offers. He made the packets simple and easy to fill out. By doing that on the front end, he cut down on the time it takes technicians like him to review the forms. Over the next year, a cohort of line-level employees like Leo implemented nearly 50 different innovations and dropped the average wait time from three hours to 15 minutes.

Loucks says the morale in her office is better now. Employees go to happy hour at the end of the day. When she arrives in the morning, she sees them joking with one another.

She did make one other change, though. To save money, she got rid of the frozen yogurt machine. Her customers may not have minded. Turns out, if you're only in line for eight minutes, you don't have time for fro-yo.

When we first launched Peak, we focused on measuring hard savings and soft savings. Hard savings were opportunities where Denver could reduce costs and save actual dollars. Soft savings were opportunities to reduce the labor hours it takes to deliver a service. The case of the frozen yogurt taught us something. We needed a way to quantify the impact of lousy service to our customers. If we made them wait for eight hours, it didn't show up in our hard or soft costs, but we knew there was a cost nonetheless. Every time we made a citizen wait for hours to get a license, we eroded his faith in government. (And at least in this case, there was also a more concrete cost to the citizens: The nearby parking meters had a two-hour limit, so our very own parking cops were handing out $25 tickets to people stuck waiting in our lines. Now *that's* customer service.)

What we realized in working with Excise and Licenses was that some of our improvements saved time for the customer, time he could spend working rather than waiting in our lines. Quantifying that cost isn't an exact science; we don't know the hourly pay of every citizen who waits in our line. With Excise and Licenses, we estimated that every hour a person didn't wait in line was worth $25 in productivity. (The average wage in Denver is $25 an hour.) By considering value to the customer, we wanted to demonstrate that results can be felt by both the city and by the customer.

Today, quantifying the impact of our innovations is a core element of our program, but early on, we almost went a different direction. When I met with the management team after being hired to work at the Peak Academy, they wanted to create a culture program. I remember thinking, *This isn't what I signed up for.* By that point, I'd spent years in government, and I'd never heard of a culture program that actually worked. I knew that if we tried to impose a culture program on Denver employees, they'd simply dismiss the idea as just another management fad that they could outlast.

I was honest with them. "Hey, if you want a culture program," I said, "I'll quit." After a lengthy discussion, we agreed not to focus on culture. Instead, we would focus on impact. When the innovations worked, the results would speak for themselves. If, as a consequence of training thousands of employees to innovate across the city, we saw a culture change, so be it.

Evidence of impact would change the culture.

So how do we demonstrate impact? Communication, communication, communication. Our team shares stories and data on a regular basis to encourage people to keep innovating. We create impact statements, which we now call "bright spots" in honor of Chip and Dan Heath's book, *Switch*. The bright spots are about 300 words long and highlight a specific innovation by one of our Green Belts or Black Belts. Sometimes they include a quote by the Peak graduate who executed the innovation, and sometimes they're written by a graduate herself. We also had newsletters and monthly Peak progress reports, with graphs about where our team is relative to hitting our goals. Lately, we've replaced those longer forms of communications with weekly blog posts. (You can read those at denpeakacademy.com.)

All these modes of communication try to convey how Peak enables employees to make their jobs better. We're not asking people to believe in some new-age philosophy. We're asking them to fix what bugs them. When they run into trouble, we'll be there to help. That's why it works.

So forget the fro-yo. Forget trying to force culture change. Focus on results.

First and foremost,
Peak is definitely not
a suggestion box.

CHAPTER 5

WHAT PEAK ISN'T

I just told you that Peak is not a culture-change program. But there are a couple other things it's not. And it's important to think about them, because if you initiate your own Peak program—believe me—you're going to run into people who expect all sorts of things that you're not set up to provide.

For starters, Peak is not a suggestion box. To illustrate what I mean, let me tell you a story about bathroom hand dryers.

A few years ago, I was in my office when I got a call from a city attorney. "Hey," said the woman on the other end, "I hear you're the guy to call to fix anything in the city."

That's a hell of a title, I thought. *Did I just get a promotion?*

She continued: "All the bathrooms in this building are designed wrong. You see, the paper towels are at the wrong end of each sink, so you have to walk back and forth after every time you wash your hands to pull the towels out of the dispenser. You really need to move all the paper towel rollers to the other end of the sinks near the door." She continued to talk about how terrible the bathrooms were designed and then finished with the kicker: "Plus, this is Denver! How sustainable are paper towels anyway? Shouldn't we be using air blowers?"

This was a lot to take in. "Um," I said, "so do you know what we do here in the Peak Academy?"

She said no, so I spent a few minutes explaining our purpose and mission. "Our job is to help city employees improve service delivery to the customer. We do that by teaching process improvement techniques like lean, six sigma, A3 or change management. But I am good friends with Suzi, who runs your building. She's one of our Black Belts, and I can connect you with her."

Silence. So, I went on.

"See, we have a philosophy that the people who do the work are the people who should work on the innovation. Suzi is really cool. I am sure she will listen to you. The other issue you may have: We don't allow people to buy new things in their innovations. Innovations should come from what you have in front of you. Hand dryers cost money, and we don't have any money right now."

The phone got quiet. She seemed disappointed. She thought I ran a suggestion box program. And she's not alone. Dozens of other cities have called me asking about our suggestion box program and how I was able to innovate with so many suggestions. We do come across a lot of suggestions—more than 500 a year—but they come from people in our trainings, and the suggestions they make are usually ones they'll have to fulfill themselves.

The Peak team consists of great problem solvers and super smart analysts. But we're not subject matter experts. If we receive a suggestion about road striping, what the hell would we know about paint, reflection beads, industrial painting trucks and sprayers? Nothing. We'd have to defer all that knowledge to the transportation team. You know, the guys who actually paint the street.

In my more than 12 years of government experience, I've witnessed dozens of employee suggestion programs. Here's how they all tend to work: The mayor or governor or department director says, "I really care about you guys. I want to hear your suggestions on how to make our department better. So I set up a box for you to write down your ideas and tell me what you think we should do to change."

The anonymous suggestions get compiled into an unreadably large spreadsheet. More than 90 percent of them will be about how we need better food in the cafeteria and why everyone needs a government-issued car. Some poor assistant spends months combing through the spreadsheet before giving the best suggestions to the department director. And then: Nothing. Nothing changes.

That's why we don't operate a suggestion box. Instead, we ask people to take responsibility for their work and to make changes in their own working environment. So stop telling other people how they should do their job. Worry about your job and fix what bugs you.

Here's something else Peak isn't: It's not a bonus program.

For several years, we toyed with the idea of doling out performance bonuses for people who innovate above and beyond their jobs. I've had lots of conversations about it with the budget director; he controls the purse strings, so he could push for a bonus program if he thought we could afford it. Several innovation programs around the country use bonuses or incentives to encourage members of their teams to innovate. Some of the programs actually provide the innovator with a percentage of any savings she helps find.

But not in Denver.

We decided against doing this a while ago. Here's why: If innovation is a bonus, then would people innovate all the time or only to get a reward? If we want to create a thousand innovators, do we need to pay them to find cool innovations? How would we structure the bonus? Would it be part of the cost savings you identified? If so, would that encourage employees to only focus on big-ticket savings, ignoring all the small solutions that could save an hour here or a few bucks there?

We decided not to have bonuses because we didn't want to send the message that innovating was an extracurricular activity. Employees need to see that innovation is part of everyone's job. When we don't expect innovation, work becomes a paycheck, not an expression of someone's passion. In the public sector, where most employees are driven by the mission of helping people, we need people to improve their work for the sake of that overarching mission.

Offering bonuses for innovation means that innovation isn't a core responsibility—it's extra work some people can volunteer to do in their spare time. And that's not the message we want to send.

Peak is also not intended to be a weapon. We teach people to focus on their own outcomes, not other people's outcomes. I'm reminded of the time I got a call from someone in Denver Human Services who had returned from a weeklong vacation to find that his desk had been completely reorganized by someone who'd gone through our training. Can you imagine? Leaving for vacation and coming back to find all your papers had been reshuffled and refiled by one of your coworkers?! But it was true. Someone I had trained used all our techniques to eliminate what he saw as his colleague's waste. He used our tools against a coworker.

Our goal at Peak isn't to train people to become giant pains in the ass to their colleagues. We don't want our Black Belts to fan out across the city slapping pink Post-its on every kind of waste or inefficiency they see on a coworker's desk or vehicle. This is not about you telling your coworkers how to do their job.

After the paper-filing incident, the Peak instructors decided to change the way we were teaching. We had to explain to people the power they have when they are equipped with process improvement tools, and the dangers of misusing that power. We tried a few different ways to show why process improvement isn't about empowering you to fix someone else's work, or to point out someone else's flaws. The one that worked the best was to just tell the story about the cleaned-up cubicle.

Why were these fleet vehicles rearranged in the middle of the night, every single night? Great question!

CHAPTER 6

SWEAT (AND CELEBRATE) THE SMALL STUFF

Sometimes it's the little things. It's the small innovations that can transform a process—and the small questions that can cause you to reexamine the way something's always been done. When you're looking for an opportunity to innovate, think small, and ask yourself this question: Is there anything you do just because it's always been done that way? If it wasn't done that way, if you could start from scratch, could you come up with something better?

Let me give you an example. Up until a couple years ago, about 50 employees from the Denver's Right of Way Enforcement would come to work each day, go into the garage and start hunting blindly for their work vehicles. I know that sounds funny, but it's completely true. Here's why: Every night around 1 a.m., the graveyard supervisor would hop into dozens of Right of Way vehicles and move them to the bottom floor of the parking garage to make room near the ground-level entrance for employees from other agencies coming to work the next morning. All of these Right of Way Enforcement vehicles look the same, and they all have the same security system, so walking around the garage frantically pressing the alarm button—while 50 of your coworkers do the same thing—accomplishes nothing. Well, it causes a symphony of alarms to go off in a confined space with surprisingly good acoustics. But it doesn't help you find your car.

Employees would go through this absurd, frustrating process

every morning. I know what you're thinking: "This is stupid. I know how to solve this. Why would any adult need help to solve a silly problem like this?"

Well, because solving this problem wasn't a central part of these employees' jobs. These were parking enforcement workers. Their job is to make sure residents pay the parking meter and don't park in a handicapped space unless they've got a permit. None of them wanted to take time away from their real jobs to deal with the car-search issue. Originally, there were only 20 vehicles, so the search didn't take all that long and it wasn't all that bothersome. As the city grew, so did our fleet and so did our team—and so did the morning search for the cars.

We worked with parking enforcement staff to brainstorm dozens of ideas on how to locate vehicles and make it easy for employees to find them. Here are some of their suggestions:

- Assign parking
- Paint names on the garage floor by each spot
- Stop moving cars around
- Put a flag on top of the car
- Use a production board with the location of the vehicle

In the end, the team came up with 21 different ways to solve the problem. Ultimately, we decided to stop moving the cars and work with the parking garage team to make some new tandem spaces. This simple change meant a little less frustration for each employee each morning. It also saved each team member several minutes a day. But when 50 people are each wasting several minutes a day, those lost minutes turn into hours. In our experience, time lost finding vehicles is a drain on employees across government, not just in Right of Way Enforcement.

I bet the example above sounds forehead-slappingly simple to you, but we see these challenges in government all the time: A particular process develops over the years, and no matter how cumbersome or asinine it gets, we don't step back to examine it and think about how we could make it better.

There's a downside to updating systems and moving beyond the way you've always done something: People tend to focus on how silly it was that the update hadn't happened sooner, or that the old way had ever been standard practice. To an extent, I understand that reaction. Why should we go out of our way to reward organizations for abandoning stupid, dysfunctional processes? But I've been doing this long enough to know that every organization has stupid, dysfunctional processes. If we dismiss those seemingly small achievements, we're creating an environment that discourages innovation. We're allowing the stupid dysfunction to persist.

One of my favorite Peak innovations received exactly the kind of tepid initial reception I'm describing. Here's what happened: A group of employees from the controller's office took a four-hour training from us. The next day, one of them, a guy named Chris Tubbs, sent me an email with the subject, "What is this report?" He attached an A3, one of those worksheets I talked about in Chapter 2. In nine steps, Chris spelled out something he wanted to change, what the target state would be and how he proposed reaching the target state.

Here's what I learned from Chris's A3: For years, the controller's office had been emailed a daily report from one of its vendors. Every day, the office would receive the report and print it out. We're not talking about a couple sheets of paper. Each day's report was about 500 pages long. But here's the kicker: Chris's team only needed the information contained in the final six pages of the report. So every day, they'd hit Print, wait for the report to print out, flip to the last six pages and toss the other 494 pages in the recycling bin. It was the height of inefficiency, and it was costing the city about $5,000 a year.

Oh, I know what you're thinking right now. You know how to solve this problem. Yes, I caught you. You're saying, *Just tell the printer to only print the last six pages!* In theory, yes, that should work. But in practice, people would forget, and the entire report would get printed out. At Peak, we encourage people to mistake-proof the process. In the case above, that meant finding a solution that never resulted in printing 494 unnecessary pages.

Again, a simple innovation won the day: Chris's team asked the vendor to stop sending the entire report and only send the pages they cared about. Then they wouldn't have to print the entire thing. If the report only has the six pages, you can't print more than you need.

When I received Chris's email, I was really impressed. I thought it was a keen innovation that should be celebrated. A couple days later, I was out with some friends who work in the private sector, explaining the type of work that Peak performs. I proudly mentioned Chris's innovation. My friends gave me a look. "Dude, only in government would someone get away with that type of stupid thing," one of my friends told me. "And only in government would you be excited about it."

There are two ways to respond to every innovation. You can roll your eyes and say, "Why didn't you do that before?" Or you can support that innovation no matter how big or small, whether it succeeds or fails. The more celebrating, the better. The more you support innovations, the more you will see them happen.

So, yes, we celebrate not printing a report. We even bought Chris and his entire team a Starbucks gift card. When you celebrate the small innovations, the big innovations become easier and easier. The truth is, incremental improvements add up. They sometimes even pave the way for a breakthrough change.

You can't spell "innovative solutions for public-sector efficiency" without an "F."

CHAPTER 7
THE F-WORD

We've talked about some of the successful innovations we've seen people implement after participating in Peak.

Now I want to talk about failures.

Failed innovations are a big part of who we are. Recognizing failures—and learning why they happened and how they might be avoided—is vital.

In our first year of the academy, trainees identified about $11 million in potential savings. The next year, it was even higher, about $12 million. We all felt pretty good about how we were going to save the city money while delivering better service. All we had to do was implement the ideas our graduates already proposed. Easy, right? I bet you know where this is going. We checked back with our graduates to see how many innovations they had actually executed, and what money they had actually saved. In the first year, they had actualized $3.8 million in savings. In the second, it was slightly better, but still only about $5.4 million. So much for easy.

We call this our "hit rate," the amount of actualized savings out of identified savings. Even in our second year, our hit rate was barely 40 percent. The discrepancy between what we *could* be saving and what *we were* saving kept me up at night. Why weren't people's innovation ideas translating into action? Anecdotally, we know at least four factors contributed to the low hit rate:

- The innovation idea would take too much time;
- It's a flawed idea;
- It's out of your control; or
- It's hard to sustain.

Let's take a look at each of these four factors, and how we might get around them.

Time. Sometimes people know they could do their work faster, but they would have to spend time up front reorganizing their daily process. The immediate sacrifice of slowing down their service delivery is just too high.

We see this a lot. An agency will go through Peak, the directors and staffers seem genuinely committed to the goals, and they're united on the innovations they want to implement. Then, months later, we learn that nothing has happened. Why?

Because the innovations took too much time to try. It's a common scenario among government agencies: An office is already swamped with work, and stepping back to implement a new innovation means taking frontline employees off the counter for hours at a time to brainstorm solutions. In the short term, productivity would actually get worse. Often, department heads decide it's safer to just keep working at the same pace they have been rather than take the time to implement an improvement.

Backlogs require many incremental changes over months, if not years. You have to be willing to trade time now reacting to the crisis in order to dig yourself out of the crisis in the long run. If you're not willing to make time for improvement, then you're choosing to keep a failing system. That might sound like the safer option, but consider how your customers would view that decision. Put another way, how would you explain your choice to the citizen waiting in the line that still takes way too long?

A flawed idea. When people go through our training, we tell them not to suggest innovations that involve new hires or new technology. Both take money. We're in government. We don't have any.

Every so often, we get someone like Jose in a class. Jose came into the training knowing exactly what problem he wanted to solve and how he was going to solve it. He worked in the accounting office, and he wanted to upgrade the software he and his coworkers used. He knew that better technology would reduce the time his team spent on their daily tasks. After the training, he came back to his boss and announced that he had some good news: He knew how to improve efficiency.

"That's great!" his boss said. "How do we do it?"

"All we have to do," Jose said, "is buy an upgrade for our existing software."

His boss stared at him. "Jose, the upgrade costs $200,000. We can't do that."

Because Jose's idea required increased spending, it went nowhere. Jose had also made another mistake that's common with Peak graduates. He went into training believing he had already arrived at the best solution. He wanted to use Peak to legitimize an idea he'd already had.

It's not always frontline workers like Jose who do that. Sometimes, it's a manager who has a flawed innovation idea. One manager came to us and asked us to run a five-day process improvement in her department. We found that her team was responsive to the training and ready to propose improvements. But it turned out that the manager herself wasn't ready to hear their ideas.

One day, she pulled us into her office and revealed that she already had a list of possible fixes written down on a whiteboard, hidden from her own team. When we asked why she hadn't shared her ideas with her staff from the beginning, she said they weren't ready. The manager hoped to use Peak to persuade people that her solutions were the right ones. When that didn't happen, she complained to other managers that the Peak method didn't work.

Sometimes a manager's innovation idea is flawed because it's exactly the type of centralized, top-down thinking that Peak tries to upend. In Peak, the widget-maker is the expert, not the widget-maker's boss. When you're trying to fix a process, you need to listen to the expert.

Out of your control. A lot of trainees think they could improve service delivery tomorrow if only their bosses or their coworkers changed. In the early days of Peak, we actually let them try. You would not believe the number of people who came through our program wanting to change the HR on-boarding process. Without getting bogged down in the details, they wanted it to take less time to start their jobs. But many of these people don't work in HR. They work for Parks or Budget or some other agency. They have no leverage in changing an HR process. When they went back to their office, they realized they had no way to turn their ideas into reality. No one at HR wanted their memo, so I got it instead. That's where their carefully considered innovation would die—because I don't work in HR either.

Let's not pick on HR. Really, this happened all over the place, and not just with people from one agency complaining about another agency. People used to finish our training and try to convince their manager or coworker to change the way they do things. But here's a newsflash: Folks don't really like being told that the way they're doing things is wrong. (Remember the guy whose coworker reorganized his desk while he was on vacation?) Again, in those instances, the ideas developed in Peak training would just sit on a piece of paper, going nowhere.

The truth is, an innovation that you can't implement yourself is probably a dead-end innovation.

Hard to sustain. We, the trainers, were also to blame for our low hit rate. One of our many initial mistakes was seagulling—you know, swooping in, making a lot of noise, crapping on everything and then flying off, leaving a big mess behind. In the first couple years of doing

Peak, we would meet with a group of employees, help them brainstorm solutions and then check back after one month, two months and three months. We weren't present for the implementation of ideas. We didn't help them troubleshoot when things went wrong, and they did go wrong a lot of the time. So it shouldn't have surprised us when our graduates failed to put their ideas into action.

We seagull less often now. Instead, we send one of our facilitators to embed with an agency for up to 12 months. We create a statement of work for the agency we're trying to help, and we execute it in the same way an outside consultant would perform a contract. We also established a mentoring program so that veteran Peak alumni pair with new graduates to provide ongoing support as they attempt to implement their first innovations. We'll explain more about the mentoring program in the next chapter.

Thanks to what we learned from our failures, we've greatly improved our hit rate over the past couple years. We can better anticipate upfront the kinds of innovations that will succeed, and we're better able to provide follow-through on helping implement those ideas. As I mentioned, our hit rate—the proportion of actual savings versus the potential savings we had identified—hovered around 40 percent in the first couple years of the Peak program. Now we've been able to steadily increase that rate. Our graduates are setting more realistic benchmarks, and meeting them. In 2015, the gap between our actualized savings ($4.4 million) and identified savings ($4.7 million) was much smaller.

There are tons of legitimate reasons why an innovation might fail. We've talked about four big ones, but I'm sure you can think of others. The point is, they do fail. You stand a better chance of succeeding if you: Accept some short-term lost time and productivity while you re-engineer your flawed process; choose solutions that are inexpensive and within your control; and have a support crew of trainers and veteran innovators to help when you hit obstacles.

Implementing change is so much easier when you work with someone who's done it before.

CHRISTOPHER STARK

CHAPTER 8

WON'T YOU BE MY MENTOR?

Innovating can be a lonely business. You may work alongside 13,000 other city employees, as I do. But when you're trying to change the way the city operates, it can feel like you're out there all alone. You look around at your team and see that no one else is trying to improve the current condition. That's frustrating, and it can cause you to stop trying to implement innovation yourself. The loneliness means people get stuck in the status quo.

When we first started the Peak Academy, we saw this type of loneliness in dozens of our Black Belt graduates. They spent five days with employees from across the city, energized about making a change, only to return to their department with no support or encouragement to keep going.

In order to combat the loneliness of a government innovator, our team researched programs that cultivate innovation. We settled on a mentoring program, which we called Peak Performers. It's partly inspired by addiction recovery programs.

No, I'm serious.

See, recovering drug addicts tell a story that goes something like this: A man falls into a hole and can't get out. A doctor passes by and the man calls up, "Doc, can you help me out?" The doctor writes him a prescription for pain relief and then leaves. A few minutes later, a priest passes by and the man calls up again, "Father, I'm stuck in a hole; can you help?" The priest kneels by the hole, prays for the man and walks away. Then the man sees a friend passing by. "Hey man!" he says. "Can you help me? I'm stuck down here and I can't get out." Without hesitation, the friend leaps into the hole. The man says, "Why'd you do that? Now we're both down here." And the friend smiles and says, "Yeah, but I've been here before, and I know the way out."

Addicts identify with the man in the hole because addiction can sometimes feel that way. You feel all alone, and the help you're offered isn't the help you need. To escape, you need an experienced peer, someone who has hit the same frustrating barriers and felt the same hopelessness. What you need isn't a one-time fix, but an ongoing relationship, a friend who will climb into the hole and walk with you through the escape route.

For us in the public sector, that metaphor works on another level. In government, the status quo is a kind of addiction. It's safe. You know what you're going to get. Innovating or changing means opening yourself up to risk, and fear of failing overcomes the rationale for trying something different. At Peak, we are not satisfied with the status quo. The status quo is what creates eight-hour waits for business licenses and six-day turnarounds for food stamps. The status quo may be familiar, but it's often unacceptable, too. That's why we embrace risk for the sake of long-term improvement.

To help you break out of the status quo, you need support. Which brings me back to the mentor program. In 2015, we began assigning all our trainees a mentor, someone who had been through the innovation process before and could help guide new Black Belts through their own innovations. It has absolutely helped more trainees put their innovations in place. Today, we see twice as many innovations submitted by Peak graduates who have mentors. Without a mentor, a Peak graduate will actualize around $1,000 in savings to the city. A Peak graduate with a mentor? Well, they actualize on average more than $5,500 in savings. Yes, that's twice as many innovations and five times the savings when we provide a mentor to a graduate.

Take Kent, a recent graduate of our Black Belt training. A week after he took the class, we connected him to a mentor, a previous Black Belt named Bill. When the two of them sat down to talk, Kent told Bill he was frustrated. Every time he proposed a new idea in his office, his manager would reject it.

Bill had had a similar experience. He'd left our training and tried to execute the innovations he'd developed. And he too had been told no by his supervisor. Bill told me he thought his supervisor was wary of his ideas, that Bill had simply discovered a way the boss was failing. Instead of seeing an opportunity to improve, the supervisor thought Bill was attacking the way she managed her team.

Based on his experience, Bill worked with Kent on strategizing a new approach. Kent used the Peak Academy's A3 framework to describe the current state and future state of the processes. Kent kept his focus on the future state—the way things could be—rather than pointing out problems with the current state. When he framed the discussion around outcomes, his supervisor began to listen. He started supporting Kent's ideas. Ultimately, Kent was able to implement two of his three innovations, thanks to his mentoring relationship with Bill. Bill jumped into the hole with Kent, and they found a way out together.

Pilot programs are a great way to test out new ideas before they fully take flight.

CHAPTER 9
PILOTS ARE MY CO-PILOT

You know something needs to change when people have been annoyed by it for years. For Heather Darlington, that something was the monthly printed notices that her department, the Denver Employees Retirement Plan (DERP), mailed to members. When DERP was formed in 1963, it would send checks to retired public employees as part of their pensions. By the 1990s, the agency could deposit checks directly into people's checking accounts, but a local ordinance still required DERP to send paper statements in the mail.

Here's what really bugged Heather: She knew she had email addresses for several thousand members and didn't need to keep printing and mailing notices. They could receive an electronic notice instead. So after attending a Peak training, she pitched an idea to her boss: Why not email notices to members who have email addresses?

Her boss was tentatively supportive. He agreed that the extra printing and mailing added up to an unnecessary expense, but he worried about backlash from members who liked their printed copy of the notice. He was mindful of forcing an unwelcome change, and Heather understood his concern. For a lot of our graduates, this is where the attempt at innovation ends. The would-be change agent returns to her department, encounters a barrier—probably the same barrier that has stifled change in the past—and gets discouraged.

Darlington took a different approach. She kept discussing the idea with her boss. Meanwhile, she worked with DERP's general counsel to draft new language in the ordinance that would allow for electronic statements. When the city council did its annual review of laws related to DERP, the general counsel introduced the proposed changes. The amendment still allowed people to receive paper statements, but it didn't require paper to be the only possible mode of communication. Even then, Heather and her boss were cautious. She convinced him to let her test a batch of emails on several hundred members (out of about 3,500 for whom they had email addresses on file). She offered them the option to go paperless, but left the decision up to them.

"If there had been a backlash," Heather says, "there was a good chance the whole thing would have been shut down." She and her boss both braced for a raft of angry phone calls and emails. To this day, her boss describes that first test phase as walking around the city with an umbrella, waiting for the rain to fall. It never did. "If anything, we got calls thanking us for being mindful of costs," Heather says. Encouraged by the initial feedback, they rolled out the rest of the batches on an accelerated schedule. Today about a third of the retirees receive paperless notices, and Heather expects the number to keep going up as DERP collects email contact information from more of its members.

In our line of work, pilots are a critical tool. They can serve as a bridge, particularly when the change being proposed is dramatic. Heather used a small pilot to make sure her idea wouldn't bring about unintended consequences. Fortunately for her, what she and her boss learned was that some customers actually preferred paperless notices. By running the experiment, she had real data to reference when arguing for an expansion of her idea. She could calculate actualized savings from not printing and mailing the notices. By the end of the first year, she saved DERP more than $45,000 in annual mailing costs. As more retirees participate, that number will go up.

The DERP example notwithstanding, pilots are exceedingly rare in city government. To the extent that they ever happen, it's not the municipal worker proposing and designing the experiment. It's usually a consultant. We should run more pilots. We have the subject-matter expertise. We spend years learning about local policies and regulations. We have improvement ideas, too.

In the past year, Peak has expanded our use of pilots by working with the Behavioral Insights Team, a private firm that applies lessons in research about human behavior to program operations. With their help, we've tested different ways of communicating with citizens to see which approach prompts the biggest response.

We used pilots to get more people to pay their vehicle registration online, rather than visit in person. We sent a few different variations of emails to citizens, with slightly different wording about paying their fees online. We found that the cheekiest message was also the most effective. It read, "I would rather be waiting in line at the DMV over the holidays ... said no one ever." This silly line increased people visiting Denver government's mobile website by 17 percent. Because of that pilot's success, the DMV is trying other fun messages to encourage more customers to register online.

Keep in mind that pilots help us identify ineffective strategies too. We tried to increase the percentage of businesses that pay their taxes online. We ran two pilots with a small subset of businesses. Sadly, one of them didn't work—the control group filed online just as much as the group that received our creative emails. In the other pilot, though, we were able to increase businesses filing online by nearly 3 percent. Both trials were useful. With the successful intervention and the failed one, we learned what worked and what didn't before scaling it up to all businesses.

Denver's Human Services Department made incredible efficiency improvements—without spending a dime.

BENJAMIN RASMUSSEN

CHAPTER 10
WORK WITH WHAT YA GOT

By now you should be familiar with one of the cardinal rules of Peak: The innovations you propose can't require new resources. If your big idea is to hire a whole extra army of frontline workers to help expedite a given process, it's going nowhere, and you should probably question your own creativity. But you'd be surprised at the kind of innovation you can achieve using the same resources you already have. Just ask Penny May.

When Penny started as the director of Denver Human Services in 2011, she had her hands full. Employees felt defeated. They wanted to help people in need, but the department's clunky processes were getting in the way. It took days to provide food stamp benefits; it took more than a year to certify someone as a foster parent. Making a child support payment could take more than an hour of standing in line (and that was the only way to make a payment, because the department hadn't set up any other way to accept them).

The economic downturn had made things even worse. As thousands of new people needed help, Human Services was overwhelmed. The lobby would fill up by the hundreds, and some people spent an entire day waiting for their turn. (Often, they were then told to return days later for an actual intake appointment.) Obviously that kind of a delay puts a strain on the applicant: He needs help now, but he's being told it will be days or weeks before he receives any real assistance.

Such dysfunction also has a huge impact on the Human Services staff. These are people who joined city government to help provide aid to those in need. The disconnect between the department's purpose and its practice causes those employees to devalue their own abilities, and it distances them from their mission.

So Penny stepped back to look at the big picture. The system itself was failing. No amount of overtime was going to resolve the long wait times. No pep talk or mission statement was going to help the team meet with everyone waiting in that lobby. Penny and her team sent their employees to the Peak Academy. They took a long, hard look at their processes and discovered some areas where they could innovate. They started by walking through the actual process of filing a new application: where it went, who signed off on it, who reviewed it and who gave it final approval. The team found that applications were stopping in multiple different mail rooms and two different floors of the building across three office locations. Each application made more than two dozen stops, requiring sign-off from a total of seven different people. The Peak trainees also noticed that the procession of new clients in the lobby wasn't a steady stream. They tended to arrive in waves, often with incomplete or redundant information that required extra work, an influx that would overwhelm the intake team and cause them to fall further and further behind throughout the day.

The team went back to the department and spent the next six months making changes to the process. They redesigned the application review process. They instituted a "blitz" system for dealing with surges in new clients: When a wave of applicants showed up, the team would call a "blitz" and pull every one of the eligibility staff out of their cubicles and relocate down to the lobby, where they could better handle the higher numbers of clients. The results were stunning. A process that used to take five days now takes less than one. Sometimes it's even completed in one *hour*.

And the really amazing thing is that the department didn't hire any new employees. They didn't make any new investments, and they didn't purchase new software (although they did find ways to use their current software system to capture better data and allow them to make better-informed decisions). All the improvements occurred because the team redesigned the work and how it flowed through the building.

The newly efficient system has taken some getting used to for the clients. After the department implemented the changes, an older man came in with an application. He had a large backpack with him and several things to read while he waited. He took a seat and settled in. But about 45 minutes after he'd arrived, his number was called, and he walked up to the counter. The eligibility worker accepted his application and told him to wait a little bit for an interview. About an hour later, his number was called again and he was provided food subsidies from a caseworker right there on the spot.

The man slumped back in his chair and began crying. "Are you okay?" the staff member asked. "I'm fine," he told her, crying from relief and happiness. "I just don't know where to eat the lunch I brought with me today." He had brought enough food and supplies with him to wait for more than eight hours, and he expected it would be days before he actually got any help. Instead he was leaving in two hours with assistance in his pocket.

Our services had become so infamous that people were packing lunch just to deal with our lines. When that man left the waiting room, uneaten lunch in hand, we had raised expectations for both the customer and the employee. On the customer side, people were receiving the help they needed, when they needed it. On the employee side, workers saw that they could make immediate and meaningful improvements in citizens' lives. Government's capacity to perform went up in the eyes of the customer, but also in the eyes of the frontline practitioners who felt a greater sense of pride in their work. And they didn't spend a dime.

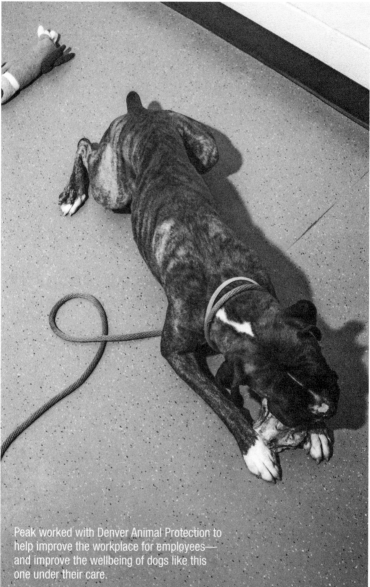

Peak worked with Denver Animal Protection to help improve the workplace for employees—and improve the wellbeing of dogs like this one under their care.

BENJAMIN RASMUSSEN

CHAPTER 11

A VIEW FROM THE TRENCHES

About a year after launching the Peak Academy, we realized that some agency heads were hungry for some kind of longer term assistance. So we created Peak Partnerships, a six- to 12-month consulting project in which a Peak team member embeds with an agency and provides daily support. Our first partnership was with the Animal Protection Division. This was a departure from our typical trainings and one-off improvement events, but we've found that partnerships can actually generate more changes with longer-lasting success.

As we say all the time, we at Peak believe the people who do the work are the true subject matter experts. In that spirit, we asked our facilitator, Melissa Field, to write about her experience launching our first Peak Partnership project. The following is Melissa's story of that partnership, in her own words.

I visited Denver Animal Protection for the first time on a cold April morning in 2013 to assist with a training. I had just started with Peak and was new to city government in general. I'd been immediately struck by how disengaged and hostile some of the employees seemed to be, and I had tried not to let it dampen my excitement for the job. This particular class was no exception. As the training got under way, they glanced at their phones and doodled on their notebooks. I sat in the back row and waved when introduced. The employees looked at me the way a clique of friends looks at an unwelcome transfer student.

When the class broke into smaller groups to practice process mapping, I wandered between groups, offering chipper suggestions. "Great job!" I said. "Don't forget to include the time spent on each step!"

One employee looked me up and down. "It's a little cold to be wearing a dress," she said.

Clearly, this wasn't going to be easy.

I had been told that Animal Protection was one of the worst teams in the city. That the department was a mess, filled with disorganized, disengaged workers. I soon found a champion in Alice Nightengale, the newly appointed director. She had heard all the same things I had— the team has several HR issues, the employees are outwardly fighting, the processes haven't changed in years. But unlike so many high-level leaders, Alice was willing to ask for help. While other departments were denouncing Peak as Mayor Michael Hancock's newest red bouncy-ball, Alice ignored the naysayers and invited Peak into every facet of the operations. "I wasn't about to turn down any help," she told me. "There were so many problems. Refusing help would have felt irresponsible to the employees, to the animals, and to the community."

What soon became clear to me was that the Animal Protection department didn't have a personnel problem; it had a *process* problem. Take, for example, the amount of time animals were being kept in the shelter. The fact is, animals were being boarded for too long. And the longer an animal stays in a shelter, the more likely that animal is to deteriorate behaviorally. Simply put, staying in a kennel for a prolonged period of time can turn a good dog bad. There are other issues with long stays, including the spread of infectious diseases. In Denver's worst-case scenarios, animals were staying at the shelter for months only to be euthanized due to deterioration.

These scenarios were breaking the staff. They stayed after-hours or even spent their lunch breaks sitting in kennels with the animals, providing extra attention and doing whatever they could to halt behavioral decline. The process was broken, turning great employees into over-worked colleagues caught in endless bouts of conflict and frustration.

In January 2014, nine months after that initial disastrous training session, Brian pitched an idea to Alice and me: I would work at Animal Protection for six months. In that time, I would train every employee in process improvement and help the staff apply that knowledge in the pursuit of shorter animal stays and reduced costs. The goal was to find $1 million in savings. I was initially against it. Finding a million bucks in savings seemed like a ridiculous proposition, considering the department operated on just under $4 million annually. I had never been a part of such a large-scale organizational change effort, and I assumed it would be impossible. Brian, however, wouldn't hear it. He told me to figure it out and deliver.

So Alice and I sat down to formulate a six-month plan. She especially wanted to come up with innovations around the animal intake process and the way administrative citations were handled. Addressing those processes—plus, let's not forget, finding $1 million to save—would take some serious investment in time and energy. But the department's employees were already so overworked that it would be nearly impossible to pull them off the floor for a day of training, let alone an entire weeklong facilitated project. Recognizing that not everyone would have the time to take the full training, Alice decided to require that each employee participate by completing at least one innovation.

The one-innovation-per-employee idea went over like a lead balloon. When the employees learned that I'd be at Animal Protection for six months, and they'd be required to submit an innovation and possibly participate in larger events, they shut down. They asked what they'd done wrong. To them, I was an auditor sent in to showcase their flaws. At staff meetings, they sat on the other side of the room from me. It felt like we had regressed to that first day when I was treated like an outcast.

For several months, I didn't hear much from the employees. I started to get nervous. Out of desperation, I decided to go off script and toss out my pre-formulated process improvement questions. Instead, I shadowed nearly every employee. I did ride-alongs with the animal protection officers and got up at 5 a.m. with the animal care attendants. I picked up poop and soggy bits of food; I chased stray dogs. And I asked every question I could think of. I asked people what they liked about their jobs, what they didn't like, and what they would change if they could. I asked them which employees at the department they trusted the most and why. I asked about their families and hobbies. I asked them where they found value and passion in life.

For a while it didn't feel like I was accomplishing much. But I reasoned that if they felt that I understood and respected them, they might trust me enough to try an innovation. I made it my mission to come to the office each day and be optimistic and compassionate, despite whatever opposition I encountered.

Then one day Audrey Borsick showed up at my office. I had spent months passing Audrey in the hall. She was in her early twenties and in a line-level animal care position. She rarely smiled, never said "hi" first, and usually avoided eye contact.

"Hey," she said glumly as she stood in my doorway. "I heard I have to do that A3 thing."

"Yes! Come in!" I said, pointing to a chair.

She continued to stand in the hall.

"I can help you with the template," I offered.

"Yeah, well, I already filled it out and emailed it to you," she said.

I opened her template and saw that she had filled it out perfectly. Her innovation idea: to track how many treats volunteers and staff gave to animals. At the time, animals were actually getting sick from too many treats. Under Audrey's proposal, the team would start using a treat tally sheet in every kennel. This would reduce the overall cost of treats and time spent caring for animals with upset tummies.

"Audrey, this is amazing!" I said. I wanted to hug her for being the first to innovate and to give me hope. But she clearly wasn't the hugging type.

"I have a lot of ideas," she said.

"Why haven't you shared them?" I asked.

She shrugged. "I didn't think anyone cared. No one has ever once asked what I thought."

After that, the ideas poured in. Other people started submitting innovations. I noticed that the best ideas came from employees who, on the surface, had seemed the most disengaged. They came from the employees who had been treated the worst, who felt discouraged, and who were disappointed from years of the status quo. They also came from every section, every age, and every level of income and education. The good ideas didn't discriminate.

By the end of the year, every single employee at Denver Animal Protection—almost 50 in all—implemented at least one innovation. Some were as small as cleaning their cluttered desks, but others had big and immediate impacts on the health of our animals and the cost of their care. Collectively, the team reduced length of stay from an average of 14 days to eight days. And yes, they saved $1 million.

Don't get me wrong. It was tough. We thought it would take six months to turn around, but it took a year. For every success, there were countless failures, and it never stopped feeling like a rollercoaster. Even today, people around the city still tell me areas where Animal Protection needs to improve. That doesn't matter, because I've learned that criticism without support is lazy at best and cruel at worst. It's the reason why we lose our best employees. Peak is about seeing the value in people on their worst days and being patient and brave enough to risk our own careers by jumping into the trenches with them. For me, this is what true public service is all about.

– Melissa Field, Peak Academy facilitator

Peak believes in the expertise of frontline workers.
(But you also can't ignore the person in charge.)

CHAPTER 12

THE MGMT.

When the city attorney called me to discuss reducing the time it takes for agencies to sign off on new contracts, I was pumped. Every single department in the city is affected by the time it takes to get a contract approved. It is one of those things that takes so long, sometimes you forget you have a contract.

We immediately got to work. We started researching the issue. We sent out a survey to get customer feedback. We held focus groups, and we met with customers individually. Several of the city attorney's employees took Peak trainings and followed up by deploying innovations. Eventually, one of them made a major dent in the contracting time by convincing the city council to change a law that had been causing a delay in the process. Within a year, the average contracting time had fallen by two days.

Working with the city attorney's office was a little different from our interactions with other agencies because the deputy city attorney, Shaun Sullivan, was a longtime friend of mine. Before we finished working with his office, I asked Shaun about his experience with my team. What he said surprised me.

"I felt like you and your team 'Peaked us,'" he said. "And I don't mean that in a positive way. You never asked me what I thought of our process. You went to our customers and got their feedback, but you never asked me."

It never feels good to have a friend tell you all the ways you've been an inconsiderate jerk, but the worst part was that he was right. By skipping Shaun and working directly with his boss, I had signaled that I didn't value Shaun's opinion. I'd gone to his boss because I thought it would be faster to get his boss to sign off than to spend the time working with Shaun on the process.

I talk all the time about working with subject-matter experts, the frontline workers who really know how the processes work. I still have to remind myself to practice what I preach. It's tempting to think that once you get approval from an agency head, change will be simple. But so much of what we've learned in Peak is that change requires leadership from frontline workers, not their bosses.

There is one danger, however, in our focus on frontline employees: the blame game. A couple years ago, we surveyed our graduates about barriers to innovation. The No. 1 reason they gave? Their coworkers.

I was really puzzled by their answer. After having met thousands of Denver city employees who seemed genuinely interested in self-improvement and serving their community better, I just didn't believe that they were all foiling one another. Sure, every office has bad eggs. But the survey responses made it seem ubiquitous. What was going on?

You'll recall that a key tenet at Peak is that people should focus on changing things that are directly under their control. Again, remember the guy who cleaned out his coworker's desk while he was on vacation? Right. Stay in your own lane. Well, the downside to telling people to focus only on what they can control is that some people think they control very, very little. So when you ask why they haven't tried to fix a problem in their work, they shrug and say, "That's Carol's job," or, "That's above my pay grade."

At Peak, we want the frontline workers to take charge and make innovative changes. Most of them are accustomed to asking for permission for everything. It's how they've been trained. So we've seen many of our Black Belts go back to their departments and feel powerless because they believe there's very little they can change on their own. It's easier to just blame their coworkers and stay with the status quo.

We now teach employees to resist the initial temptation to assign blame and give up. We pair them up with mentors who can offer encouragement and problem-solving tips.

And I tell them this true story:

I once had a boss at the airport who liked to trade book recommendations with me. One day, she handed me a tome titled *The No Asshole Rule*, by Robert Sutton. I took the book from her and thought, *Finally! A way to deal with my coworkers!* See, I loved my job at the airport, but it was stressful, and I often complained about my colleagues. Here was my boss, not only validating my opinions about my peers but handing me a guidebook for how to deal with all those difficult people.

It wasn't until I finished reading the book that I realized it was about me.

It's easy to complain about a dysfunctional workplace and lay blame on others. The more fruitful and difficult route is to keep your focus on the positive change you can create, and not worry about the failings of those around you. The moral of the story is, if you think the reason you can't innovate is because of all the assholes you work with, then there's a good chance you might be one too.

As you can see, there's a tricky dance here between management and frontline employees. Focus too much on the supervisors in charge, and you lose out on the subject-matter expertise from the employees who are actually engaged in the work day in and day out. Spend all your attention on frontline workers, though, and you can alienate their managers, who feel like they're being shanghaied by innovation.

We've noticed a pattern with Peak graduates and their managers. Many of the employees we train return to their office and encounter hostility from their boss. Here's what happens: A Black Belt comes back and reports a handful of things he wants to change, as we require from anyone who takes one of our classes. The boss then interprets these ideas not as innovations but as insubordinate challenges of her authority. The fact that the employee is demanding improvements comes off as criticism of the boss' performance as a manager. Some of the best innovation ideas I have seen submitted to Peak were never implemented because the manager refused to acknowledge them.

The best managers give their employees the space to propose and implement change. They don't perceive employee initiatives as threats to their leadership; instead, they see them as testaments to the team's collective strength and ability to continuously improve. I try to follow these principles in the way I manage my own Peak team. During performance reviews of my facilitators, I ask them to propose three innovations for improving the Peak program. I want my staff to know that I welcome their ideas for owning and improving the program. Plus, if it goes in a performance review, they'll be more motivated to act on their ideas and achieve success.

My biggest piece of advice for any manager is to get out of the way. Stop dictating. Listen to your employees and be open to their ideas.

And my biggest piece of advice for you, if you want to create a Peak program, is to think about the whole picture. Focus on the valuable assets and ideas that your frontline employees bring to the table. But don't neglect the managers, lest they feel ambushed by the process. Don't allow your trainees to give up because they feel pigeonholed or constrained once they return to their department; help them bridge the gap with their coworkers *and* their bosses.

And, you know, don't be an asshole.

Save yourself a world of hurt:
Do your homework on the history
and context of a workplace
before you show up.

CHAPTER 13

BACKGROUND CHECKS

Have you ever walked into a party, or a dinner, and you could immediately sense there was something *off* about the atmosphere in the room? There was an electric tension buzzing in the air, and you felt like you were the only person being left out of a conversation. Then later—the next day, or the next week—you found out that the hosts had been fighting with one another just moments before you showed up.

That can happen with Peak. If you don't understand the background of the department you're walking into—if you don't know the context of the problems these employees are dealing with—things can go south. Fast.

On one occasion, we'd been brought in by the Public Works Department to conduct an executive training for some of the upper managers there. Our task was to help train people who worked in the fleet management program.

We arrived and started the first class, giving our usual spiel about process improvement and how to help employees come up with innovations. Before we knew it, the entire room pounced on us and began attacking everything we said.

"This is crap."

"What the hell is this stupid program?"

"We aren't like Toyota."

"Have you even *met* the people here?"

It got worse from there.

Now let me give you some background information that I wish I'd had at the time. As it turned out, earlier that year a group of analysts in the city had done a review of the fleet program, including things like auto parts purchasing, vehicle utilization and maintenance. The review covered all the fleet programs that were located in three different organizations: police, fire, and public works. The report, which was supposed to be confidential, somehow found its way to the fleet team. It recommended privatizing parts of the group and combining the police, fire and public works fleets into one. Combining departments, as anyone working in government knows, comes with a ton of intense fallout and resistance. Needless to say, the report had pissed off the entire department.

So yeah, I wish we'd known that before walking into the room that day. It wasn't all awful. I met some incredible people who worked in the fleet program, people who didn't want to attack us or participate in the vitriol. But the larger lesson was that we had entered into a situation we didn't understand. We should have done our research and understood why we were being asked to help—and who was doing the asking—before we began.

A year later, the fleet team invited us back. Several of their team members had gone through a five-day Black Belt training since we'd last visited the department. I had huge reservations, but I reluctantly agreed. Two of my facilitators came with me to work with the team. The conversation still started out rough. I had to remove a facilitator after one too many heated sessions got out of hand. The end result, though, was amazing. The fleet team created a plan worth about $4 million that would help the department purchase a large number of new vehicles and get them into service more quickly. The team opted to join in on a larger purchasing pool with the State of Colorado. They also agreed to stop purchasing all kinds of different types of cars and trucks and instead began to standardize the fleet, making it easier and cheaper to keep parts on hand. Incredibly smart, simple and easy to do. So ultimately, our fleet experience had a happy ending. But the moral for us was that we should never have shown up in the first place without doing our homework. You'll save yourself a lot of headaches if you do your due diligence before you walk into a new situation.

It matters where an innovation program sits within city government—but each option has pros and cons.

CHAPTER 14

ARMCHAIR POLITICS OR: WHERE TO PUT YOUR PEAK?

Peak is not a politically motivated program. Except when it is. Sometimes. Actually, let me back up.

See, there's a big difference between elected political leaders and career public servants. Politicians have a shelf life. Many of them have term limits. And even the ones who don't have limits still think in terms of a few years. The political system is one that requires short-term thinking and rewards self-promotion. Career employees are different. We don't have the same time constraints, so we're not as interested in quick wins. Many of us will be here for dozens of years. We don't need to think in terms of four years, or eight.

My boss, David Edinger, refers to this as a renter-versus-owner culture. When you're a renter, you see things in terms of crises. You want a fix, and you want it now, while you're still living in the property. The benefit of a renter's mentality is that it creates urgency. Problems cannot be ignored.

Owners have a different perspective. They've been on the property a long time. Problems that seem like a crisis to a renter seem more like a nuisance to an owner. It's not the first problem that has cropped up, and it won't be the last. Owners think about fixes in the long term, too. They plan out the roof repair, replanting the garden, remodeling the kitchen. It's not about a complete overhaul of a "broken" home. It's about small updates over months and years.

Peak falls somewhere between the renter and owner. We were born out of a mayoral initiative, so we have some of that renter's urgency. But our organizational structure places us several layers away from the mayor. (My boss is the budget director.) More importantly, the people we train, the people who are really responsible for implementing change, are owners. Many of them will likely outlast the mayor. So we're okay with incremental changes. If 13,000 city workers are making small improvements, the effect will be big.

I know that several celebrated innovation teams around the country operate out of their mayor's office. The rationale is that the mayor wields influence to make change fast. Agency heads have to listen to him or her. Because the mayor oversees the entire city, an innovation team in his office can touch every type of municipal work, from policing to garbage collection. So it makes sense that most cities leading the way in innovation right now take a strong mayoral approach.

But here's why I would argue against that structure, and what I like about our setup in Denver: When the mayor and his staff are the direct supervisors, the work will take on a political bent. It will be subjected to political timelines. The issues that innovation teams address will be political issues that are more important to the mayor than the municipal workers. Innovation works when people can fail without worrying about the consequences. Innovation struggles when consequences end up in the paper or in a meeting with the mayor's team, explaining why things went wrong.

When you place an innovation team in a political office, the team's objectives become subsumed by political objectives. Instead of frontline workers trying to untangle an internal parking or filing system that wastes their time, they become part of some grand plan to boost the local economy or end homelessness in four years. I'm not demeaning those kinds of goals; they're incredibly valuable. Mayors should do those things. I'm just saying that those big policy issues are beyond the scope of what most city workers can control on a daily basis, which is what Peak is focused on.

There's another problem, which is that people *respond* differently to a program that's based in the mayor's office. The good news is people will work with you. The bad news is they'll probably do it for the wrong reasons, they won't work in earnest, and their interest will last only as long as the leading politician's time in office. This happened to us. Early in Mayor Michael Hancock's first term, one city department received a scathing audit. The department was missing money, missing documents and areas were in visible disarray with piles of backlogged files. The mayor had an idea: The Peak team should help this troubled department clean up its processes and make other major changes in light of what the auditor found. (For all I've said about the distance we keep from the chief politician in our city, we do get calls like these and we respond, because the mayor is, you know, in charge. He's the top executive and he's given us a lot of support over the years.)

It was clear from my first meeting with the manager of that department that she wasn't interested in making real change. She didn't believe that the findings in the audit were accurate, and she didn't think there was any deep, underlying problem in need of solving. She'd agreed to work with us because she wanted to please the mayor. But to her, we were a group of executive assistants there to help organize the files. In the end, we failed at making permanent change in the department. One of the biggest struggles we've had at Peak is encountering people who don't want to change. And when we ride in like white knights on the mayor's orders, department heads are especially resistant. They accept our help because the political pressure is too great to ignore. But if that's the only reason they're employing process improvement strategies, the change won't last. Political pressure alone just doesn't have a long-term impact.

Keeping out politics is but one consideration in where to place your innovation team within your government. Sometimes, technology departments will try to own the innovation team. There's a certain logic to letting that happen. Your software experts probably understand the need to take risks, collect data, measure impact and adjust your approach based on results. But here's the downside: When a tech organization owns innovation, every idea tends to involve an enterprise technology project with a hefty price tag. Many of the best ideas we see in Peak don't involve technology at all, and it's important to create an approach that doesn't resort too quickly to buying new software.

Human resources is another common place to establish a performance and training program, and I'd advise against that, too. Performance management classes should be taught by people who have worked as frontline employees, delivering services. HR trainings tend to be taught by people whose background is in professional training. They just don't have the same experiential insights that a former parking cashier can bring.

So what about housing your Peak program in the Department of Finance, as we do in Denver? Well, that can pose issues too. If your team is constantly looking to save money and take money from other departments, then you'll fail to be a successful innovation program. Word will get out that you're just concerned with saving money and not worrying about the quality of programs or services you provide to the rest of the city.

As you can see, finding the right place for a Peak program to live can be really difficult. I happen to think that locating a program like this within the finance office is the best solution with the fewest pitfalls.

But every option comes with its own tradeoffs, and you need to be mindful of that.

To make a positive impact on the lives of residents

Every child deserves a family

To challenge myself in new ways and to change and growth

Make a difference

I love improvi governm

I enjoy helping citizens solve their problems

Feels good to help others

To be a change agent

To h peop

Improve Public Impact

Denver gave me the opportunity to pursue my passion

I live here and my family is here

Work with smart people

Becau it's a challeng

I love making things better

To Make Denver BETTER

To imp the

I believe in data & analysis

Make life better

To enhance the greater good

To Mak a dif

In most cases, public employees are already committed to the mission of government.

I want to do something that helps others

I ♡ delivering my widgets!

©STARKBELLAMYCREATIVE.COM

CHAPTER 15

SCREW BUY-IN

In Peak, we don't use the phrase "buy-in."

The language and mentality of buy-in are ubiquitous in government. Buy-in is something you do for an investment in the future. And the goal in the end is to "cash out." Think about it. You buy into a stock, a poker game, a house or some mutual fund. All these are designed to do one thing: increase your original investment so you can cash out later.

It's an approach that forces you to sell your idea to others. You try to convince people that your solution is the right solution. You might even criticize competing ideas because they threaten the sale of your idea. (I've had managers tell me they define buy-in as convincing their employees that the manager's idea was their own. That's not good management; it's manipulation. And nobody likes being manipulated.) Think about all the examples in this book. Most of them are simple changes, and many of them are incremental and complementary, building on a series of successive improvements over time.

Stay away from buy-in. Instead, work with people by creating a connection and a relationship. When your team members are connected and you have a trusting relationship, you don't have to search for the elusive buy-in.

I once worked for a boss years ago who would do everything he could to socialize his ideas to the rest of the workforce. He would call in the managers and even hold one-on-one meetings with team members in which he would discuss his ideas and how our teams needed to change. He would then end each conversation with, "What do you think?" Initially, we all gave him feedback—we told him what we thought—and then two months later he would launch his own idea without any of our changes or recommendations. After going through this exercise several times a year, we all stopped reacting to his pitches. We realized he wasn't looking for input. He was looking for us to buy into his idea and way of working. He didn't want to hear what we thought. He ran with all his ideas and then complained about how the team never bought into them.

Buy-in is cheap. What you really want is *belief*. When you want your team to get on board for your amazing innovation, you need them to *believe* in your shared mission and the need to innovate to get there. "When someone believes what you believe, they will work for blood, sweat and tears," says author and motivational speaker Simon Sinek. We at Peak agree with Sinek: Belief is so much more valuable than buy-in. (We like him so much, we show one of his TED Talks in our class.)

So how do you get people to *believe* in your innovation? By working together on the innovation process as an entire team. When you collaborate, the ideas come quickly and you'll get better results. That means respectful debate of ideas and modifying your proposals based on thoughtful feedback. You need to get to a place where people can say, "I love that idea, but what if we combined it with this other idea?" Sometimes, it takes implementing a failed idea just to find the right one—or the right six—that will work. If you're the manager, it might also mean throwing out your original solution. But the engagement you'll gain from your team is worth the sacrifice. The more people who contribute to the process, the more likely the solution will last.

Part of the problem with seeking buy-in from municipal workers is that it's redundant. They're already bought in. At the end of every week-long training, I ask people to write on a sticky note why they work where they do. Then we post all of their answers on a wall. Invariably, they say things like, "I want to make the city better" or "I want to make a difference" or "I want to make Denver a great place to live." You don't need to convince them to be committed and passionate about their work. They already are.

I recognize that as you read this, you're probably thinking this is nothing more than semantics. I disagree. When you are working as a team with a common goal—say, getting business licenses out to customers faster—you recognize that it isn't going to take just one solution. It's going to take dozens of innovations to make these changes. When it's your team members moving the innovations, they take ownership and responsibility for them. The ideas didn't come from the boss or an elected official. They were developed by the people doing the work.

Government programs like Peak are about freeing employees to perform at a higher level, to match that burning desire with new skills so that their agency moves faster and makes citizens happier. Peak provides tools to help problem solve and a platform to help get your ideas into action. When people feel as though they're getting better at what they do, and their work is helping other people, that gives them a deep sense of satisfaction.

And that's eminently more powerful than buy-in.

Eric Wolf ignored several key Peak tenets—and wound up creating an innovative new system for scheduling shared conference rooms.

CHAPTER 16

OKAY, NOW BREAK ALL OUR RULES

When Eric Wolf started his job in the city as a risk analyst, he had a problem trying to reserve a room for a large meeting with outside advisers. The city's method for scheduling meetings and reserving conference rooms was antiquated and strange. You'd hit a button, then your computer would run some weird script and then send an email to an administrator who would then check an Excel sheet to see if the room was being used. Rooms were constantly being double-booked. Many times rooms were used without reservations.

Three months after Eric took our Peak training, I ran into him and he told me he'd decided to work on the "room requestor." I said, "What the hell you are doing that for? You know the rules. You're only allowed to innovate on things within your control!" Remember, Eric is an analyst in the Finance Department. He has no sphere of influence in Technology Services. It would be like a custodian telling a physician how to suture a wound. (Or, for that matter, a doctor telling a janitor how to mop a floor.)

Anyway, we tell our trainees not to attempt innovation outside their personal work. But Eric is a stubborn millennial. He used to work at Facebook. He thinks he can change the world. And he doesn't understand the word "no." So he didn't listen to me.

Eric worked on the room requestor issue for several months. He walked the entire building and mapped all the conference rooms.

He then figured out how to use Microsoft Outlook to program all the conference rooms in the building. After that, he met with the tech services team. He presented his idea and all the work he had done.

They thanked him for his work, and then they did something that surprised me. They implemented his idea. They announced we'd be moving to Microsoft Outlook and the old room requestor system would be gone in a matter of months. Keep in mind, fixing the room requestor was never a priority for the tech team. It was far down on their to-do list. But because of Eric and his perseverance, this simple change freed up about five minutes for every employee every time they booked a room, and it saved roughly five hours a week for the person who used to approve or reject meeting requests on the old system. That's a lot of working hours the city used to spend on a system that didn't work anyway. Now those hours can be put to better use, and the new process is smoother and easier. All because Eric didn't listen to me.

Not only did Eric's idea involve a solution that was out of his control, it also involved a technological change. And as you'll recall, that goes against another cardinal rule here at Peak. When we talk about innovation, we try to completely remove technology from the equation.

Well, here's where I spill the beans: There are exceptions to our rules.

For instance, after going through our training, a team of employees at Excise and Licenses convinced their manager to purchase new desktop printers. The new printers allowed them to remain at their desk working, rather than walking all over the office to fetch printouts. Yes, here is where you recite my favorite line back to me: "Technology costs money, and we work in government. We don't have any." With the printers, however, the upgrade made such a difference in productivity and speed of service that it was worth the upfront price. Even in government.

Another example: After we trained folks in the Office of the Clerk and Recorder, they decided to develop and launch their own mobile app. We never, ever teach people to look for solutions that involve launching an app. But they did and they trademarked it. Their app allows people to gather petitions for candidates and ballot measures on a tablet computer, and it instantly checks each signature to approve or remove it. The app innovation saves the Clerk and Recorder's office scads of time, and it's also more efficient for the person gathering petitions because they know immediately whether they qualify for a ballot. So our rules aren't perfect. We still think they're good guiding principles. Innovations are most likely to succeed when they don't require new money or new technology, and when they're within your sphere of control. But, hey, rules were made to be broken. (Please don't tell my teenage daughter I said that.)

David Edinger, Scotty Martin and I started the Peak Academy, but we're doing everything in our power to make sure it doesn't end with us.

©STARKBELLAMYCREATIVE.COM

CHAPTER 17

GO FORTH AND PEAK

On a construction site, at the end of a shift, the workers can turn around and look at what they accomplished. They can say, today I built this floor, or that sidewalk, or the roof.

We don't often have that sense of accomplishment in government. Policy and public-sector improvement can be abstract forms of work. You spend hours reading, writing, studying and learning. You engage in philosophical discussions trying to get to the bottom of a difficult issue facing large numbers of people you'll never even meet. It's difficult to try to make changes to things that you cannot feel or see.

When we first ran workshops and rapid improvement events, we did what a lot of facilitators do. We grabbed a marker, walked to the front of the room, and started writing down people's comments. We were really good stenographers, but we noticed that only certain people participated in the exercises. Our wonderful scribblings represented a vocal minority in the room.

So we changed our approach. We handed over the markers and sticky notes and told the people making the suggestions to write them down and post them on the wall. We played a more passive role: We would lead them through the discussion, ask the occasional question and try not to pass judgment on anyone's ideas. It worked. More people got out of their chairs, walked up to the board and posted their ideas. The quiet types who would never call out an answer with me at the front of the room were much more comfortable contributing to the conversation by sticky note.

To me, this is fundamental to innovation: People need to touch change. And being able to touch change is a huge problem for the municipal and state employees who spend hours in office buildings with little to no direct contact with a customer. And it is a huge challenge for Peak. That's why we rely so much on employees making their *own* case for change and suggesting their *own* innovations and running their *own* changes. It's why we send all our Black Belt trainees on Gemba walk sessions. They meet the people who do the work that's been labeled as problematic; in some cases, they see the customers who suffer because the process isn't running smoothly. Change becomes real. It becomes something you can touch.

I try to think about my own work the same way. When people ask what I do, I don't talk A3s or lean concepts or gap analysis. I say, "My team helps people get stuff faster." That's tangible change. You can touch it.

Anyone who's ever started a new initiative in any organization at some point must confront the question: Will this outlast me? And in government, where we're trying to make a positive difference in people's lives, you hope it does. Twenty years from now, it'd be okay if no one knows the names of the people who started Peak. But I sure hope they're still taking trainings at the Peak Academy.

I have a big personality. Most of the time, it helps with my job. It helps with recruiting talented facilitators and convincing new people to try our classes. It helps with forming partnerships between Denver agencies and our program. But I don't ever want my people to think, "What would Brian do in this situation? What would he think?" And that goes for the original founders of the Peak Academy, too. It shouldn't be the David Edinger Program or the Scotty Martin Program or even the Mayor Hancock program. We wanted to teach Denver workers the process of continuous improvement. The program needs to be self-sustaining. It needs to outlive its founders.

This is why we focus so hard on the training of our teams. Great organizations do not rely on a superstar to lead the team and maintain their strength in the market. They make sure they train their entire team to carry on their work. To paraphrase something Cesar Chavez said, "Once you learn to read, you cannot unlearn." Even if every founding member of Peak left the city tomorrow, there would still be thousands of employees who have gone through our training. They won't unlearn the core concepts of waste elimination, process improvement and customer-driven service.

Another reason we're optimistic that the Peak Academy will have a long-lasting impact on Denver government is its many offshoots. Several Denver departments have created their own process improvement programs that work in conjunction with Peak. As of this writing, the Controller's Office, the Department of Human Services, and Denver International Airport each have their own employee-led innovation teams. We still train their staff, but then they return to the agency with their own in-house facilitators who are ready to help them realize their improvement ideas. The city library system has even started its own basic training for employees to learn process improvement techniques.

The Peak Academy is still young, but I'm optimistic about its legacy beyond Denver, too. As of this writing, we've trained more than 200 people from outside Denver government—public employees from Los Angeles to Providence, Rhode Island; from San Francisco to Kansas City, Missouri; from Gainesville, Florida, to Edmonton, Alberta.

We've talked to local agencies in many states that have expressed interest in launching their own Peak-style program.

You can create your own process improvement program. Don't be intimidated by the unfamiliar terms and the expensive certification classes. I myself have had some basic education in the field: I took a local class in lean, and I've received certification in six sigma. But I'm still not a true expert. I didn't visit Japan to see the purest form of lean in practice at auto factories. What I've found is most important is a hunger for information, a commitment to creating positive change in your organization and a willingness to fail.

We built our program through grit, fun, and trial and error. We set out to make it different from HR trainings and different from hiring an outside consultant to tell us what we were doing wrong. We wanted people to come away from our class saying, "Wow, I am exhausted, inspired, and pumped to go back to work!"

You can do the same.

Peak is what works for Denver. But it isn't paint-by-numbers. Not everything we do will apply in your city or state. Sure, you can borrow everything we post on our website and in this book (I hope you do!). But you still have to make it yours. Change the logos. Modify the terms. Celebrate success stories from your experiences and make them the anecdotes you share in classes.

I only hope you make demonstrable change in your own community. Remember: Innovate. Elevate. Repeat.

Find much more, including worksheets
and other resources, at
governing.com/peakbook

The only reason this book is possible is because of my incredible team at the Peak Academy. I am lucky so many smart and dedicated public servants took a leap with me and made this crazy idea come to life.

Front row, left to right: Kate May, Scotty Martin, Sophia Ernst, Brian Elms, Christi Ng, Greg Reger, Jerraud Coleman.

Second row, left to right: Melissa Field, Faustino Payan, Daniel Barton, Tom Chase, Chris Scarborough, Kent Lighthall.

Not pictured: Patrice Hawkins, Tanya Davis, Katie Paulson, Katherine Lyons.

ACKNOWLEDGEMENTS

In order to write a book like this, hundreds of people helped. This book could not be possible without my wife, Leslie Oliver, and my amazing daughter, Kora Elms Fleming.

Our heartfelt thanks go to Mayor Michael Hancock, David Edinger, Brendan Hanlon, and Scotty Martin for helping forge the creation of Peak. Thank you Cristal DeHerrera, Scott Martinez, and Kwali Farbes for legally making this happen. Thank you to the Peak Team: Melissa Field, Courtney Law, Jerraud Coleman, Daniel Barton, Tom Chase, Kate May, Patrice Hawkins, Katie Paulson, Katherine Lyons, Kent Lighthall, Tanya Davis, Faustino Payan, Brian Pool, Christi Ng, Chris Scarborough, and Sophia Ernst. Thank you to Greg Reger for making a fantastic class and for building our database. Thank you to all the amazing people who agreed to read this before it was published: Governor Edward G. Rendell, David Osborne, Ken Miller, Theresa Reno-Weber, Rob Christensen, JoAnn Lamphere, and Stephen Goldsmith. Big ups to the management team during this process: Stephanie Adams, Steve Bohn, Kelly Greunke, and Laura Kane Perry.

To my friends, without your help, I would never have this opportunity. You are amazing: Mary Buckley, Jenny Schiavone, Jim Pinto, Alice Nightengale, Crissy Fanganello, Jeff Lancaster, Jill Coffman, Kelly Brough, Bobby Waidler, Laura Wachter, Greg Hegarty, RJ Prushnok, Anthony Carroll, Penny May, Georgia Howard, Stephen

Krupin, Adam Smith, Doug Woods, Jeff Geller, Leo Lopez, Bill Hafner, Donna Kotake, Jon Robinson, Terri Runyan, Anthony Aragon, Erin Brown, Seth Howsden, Connie Coyle, Audrey Borsick, Eric Wolf, Loretta Bennion, Jill Jennings Golich, Amber Vancil, Chris Tubbs, Steven Zsako, Heather Darlington, Barb Puls, Shaun Sullivan, Daro Mott, Inger Brinck, Janice Sinden, Evan Dreyer, Julie Steenson, Jose Cornejo, Nicole Pollock, John Elias, Charlie Wright, Steve Hersey, Bill Riedell, Steve Hart, Brandon Lawrence, Doug Elenowitz, Tom Lisi, John E. Luehrs, Lorii Rabinowitz, Andrea Albo, John Martinez, Dolores Moreno, Bob McDonald, Amber Miller, Meghan McGrane for loaning me your husband, Patrick Kraus, Fred and Andrea Elms, Caroline Hendrickson, Steve Ellington, Gretchen Hollrah, Stacie Loucks, Paul Kresser, Patrick Heck, Abass Kamara, Dionne Williams, Mike Strott, Jon Lehmann, Chris Herndon, Brad Buchanan, Dawn Quintana, Debra Johnson, Nita Henry, Raelynn Napper, Kathleen Webb, Jessica Casey, Beth Machann, Amber McReynolds, Scott Gilmore, Emily Snyder, Bryan Moore, Tanya Osiowy, Beth Blauer, Kim Bradford, Benoy Jacob, Amanda Beach, Paul Washington, Todd Babcock, Emily Lauck, Bert Williams, Jill Ryan, Ron LeBlanc, Daniel Ballard, Marcus Pachner, Mike Braaten, Denise Hawkins, Deanne Durfee, Sam Mamet, Matt LeCerf, Carter Hewgley, Matt Raifman, Henry Sobanet, Zach Markovits, David Padrino, David Yarkin, Karla Pierce, Nora Dowd Eisenhower, Scott Piefer, Elspeth Kirkman, Suzi Latona, and Lis Costa. Thank you Tim Scull and Megan Rundlet for letting us crash at your house. I am sure I forgot someone, but just so you know, you are awesome!

Thank you Mark Funkhouser, Paul Taylor, and Paul Harney for taking a chance on this kid and loaning me J.B. Wogan and Zach Patton, who are the most amazing writers and editors the world can offer. And thank you to the owners of The Hamilton in Washington, D.C., where the idea for this book started.

We at Denver Peak Academy appreciate all the help we have received from the following organizations: Harvard's Ash Center for Democratic Governance and Innovation, TLG and the Alliance for Innovation, Behavioural Insight Team North America, Denver Health, BMGI, Simpler, Willow Tree, North Highland, What Works Cities, *Governing* Magazine, Bloomberg Philanthropies, Johns Hopkins Center for Government Excellence, National League of Cities, City Lab, University of Colorado Certified City Manager Program, and the Colorado Municipal League.

Big thank you to our photographers who made us look good: Eric Bellamy, Chris Stark, Benjamin Rasmussen and David Kidd.

J.B. would like to thank: Everyone listed above. This book is the product of your collective effort. Thanks to my wonderful wife, Meghan McGrane, who let me write a book while we planned our wedding. Thanks to my family for encouraging me to write for a living. Thanks to the entire *Governing* team who supported me throughout the project. And thanks to Rafael Carlo Jacinto Diy, whose early feedback helped us "process improve" the book.

DAVID KIDD

J.B. Wogan (left) and Brian Elms (right)

AUTHOR BIOS

Brian Elms is a founding member of Denver's Peak Academy. He was born in Denver and raised in the outlying suburbs. He graduated from Regis University and then served in the National School and Community Corps (AmeriCorps) as a team leader. He joined the Rendell for Governor campaign and later served as the Policy Director for the Pennsylvania Department of Aging. After working for AARP, Brian moved back to his hometown and served as the Assistant Director of Government Affairs at Denver International Airport. In 2012, he started working with the Peak Academy. He is a terrible snowboarder, a slow runner, and a horrible ping pong player. He has an incredibly awesome daughter and lives in Denver with his wife Leslie. Brian believes we can all change the world one innovation at a time.

J.B. Wogan is a staff writer at *Governing* magazine. He was born in Denver and grew up in the Baltimore area, where he studied public policy at Johns Hopkins University. He has written for PolitiFact and *The Seattle Times*. Most of what he knows about local government he learned as a politics reporter in Sammamish, Wash., where he covered two sewer districts, a fire district, the police department, the city council, the county council, and the state legislature. The Washington Newspaper Publishers Association named him News Writer of the Year in 2010. He lives with his wife Meghan in Washington, D.C.

FURTHER READING

Here are some books we value in the Peak Academy. Some of them have informed our ideas and our curriculum. Others are just great reads.

Bissinger, Buzz. *A Prayer for the City.* New York: Knopf Doubleday Publishing Group, 1997

Collins, Jim. *Good to Great: Why Some Companies Make the Leap... and Others Don't.* New York: Harper Collins Publishers Inc., 2001.

Collins, Jim and Morten T. Hansen. *Great by Choice.* New York: Harper Collins Publishers Inc., 2011.

Covey, Stephen M.R. *The Speed of Trust: The One Thing that Changes Everything.* New York: Free Press, 2006.

Diamond, Stuart. *Getting More: How You Can Negotiate to Succeed in Work and Life.* New York: Three Rivers Press, 2010.

Duhigg, Charles. *The Power of Habit: Why We Do What We Do in Life and Business.* New York: Random House Trade Paperbacks, 2012.

Gawande, Atul. *The Checklist Manifesto: How to Get Things Right.* New York: Metropolitan Books, 2009.

George, Bill and David Gergen. *Discover Your True North: Becoming an Authentic Leader.* New Jersey: John Wiley & Sons Inc, 2015.

Gladwell, Malcolm. *David and Goliath: Underdogs, Misfits, and the Art of Battling Giants.* New York: Little, Brown and Company, 2013.

Gladwell, Malcolm. *What the Dog Saw: and Other Adventures.* New York: Little, Brown and Company, 2009.

Grant, Adam. *Give and Take: Why Helping Others Drives Our Success.* New York: Penguin Group LLC, 2013

Grant, Adam. *Originals: How Non-Conformists Move the World.* New York: Penguin Group LLC, 2016

Heath, Chip and Dan Heath. *Made to Stick: Why Some Ideas Survive and Others Die.* New York: Random House, 2008.

Heath, Chip and Dan Heath. *Switch: How to Change Things When Change is Hard.* New York: Crown Publishing Group, 2010.

Horowitz, Ben. *The Hard Thing About Hard Things: Building a Business When There Are No Easy Answers.* New York: HarperCollins Press, 2014.

Johnson, Steven. *Where Good Ideas Come From.* New York: The Penguin Group, 2010.

Kelley, Tom and Jonathan Littman. *The Art of Innovation: Lessons in Creativity from IDEO, America's Leading Design Firm.* Doubleday: New York, 2001.

Koenigsaeker, George. *Leading the Lean Enterprise Transformation,* Second Edition. Boca Raton: CRC Press, 2013.

Kotter, John P. *Leading Change. Harvard Business Review,* 1996.

Lewis, Michael. *Moneyball: The Art of Winning an Unfair Game.* New York: Norton, 2004.

Martin, Karen and Mike Osterling. *Value Stream Mapping: How to Visualize Work and Align Leadership for Organizational Transformation.* New York. McGraw Hill Education, 2014.

McChesney, Chris and Sean Covey. *The 4 Disciplines of Execution: Achieving Your Wildly Important Goals.* New York: Free Press, 2012

Miller, Ken. *Extreme Government Makeover: Increasing Our Capacity to Do More Good.* Washington, DC: Governing Books, 2011.

Miller, Ken. *We Don't Make Widgets: Overcoming the Myths That*

Keep Government from Radically Improving (Governing Management Series). Washington, DC: Governing Books, 2008.

Osborne, David and Peter Hutchinson. *The Price of Government: Getting the Results We Need in an Age of Permanent Fiscal Crisis.* New York: Basic Books, 2004.

Ries, Eric. *The Lean Startup: How Today's Entrepreneurs Use Continuous Innovation to Create Radically Successful Businesses.* New York: Crown Business, 2011.

Sinek, Simon. *Leaders Eat Last: Why Some Teams Pull Together and Others Don't.* New York: Penguin Group LLC, 2014.

Syed, Matthew. *Black Box Thinking: Why Most People Never Learn from Their Mistakes—But Some Do.* New York: Penguin Group LLC, 2015

Thaler, Richard H. and Cass R. Sunstein. *Nudge: Improving Decisions About Health, Wealth, and Happiness.* New York: The Penguin Group, 2009.

Womack, James P. and Daniel T. Jones. *Lean Thinking: Banish Waste and Create Wealth in Your Corporation.* New York: Free Press, 2003.

DENVER PEAK ACADEMY

MISSION STATEMENT

Peak Academy trains and coaches employees at all levels to improve the way government works. Through innovation, employees do more with less and enhance the Denver city experience.

VISION

Peak – changing the way government operates to improve your experience.

MOTTO

Innovate. Elevate. Repeat.

VALUES

Peak Academy believes...

- In achieving measurable results through continuous improvement;
- In our ability to make Denver the most well-run city in the nation;
- In patience with people and impatience with processes;
- In supporting colleagues to innovate;
- In failure; because failure leads to breakthrough